ISO 14001 AND THE LAW

Legal Guide for the Implementation of the Environmental Management Standards

S. Wayne Rosenbaum

 AQA Co. ▪ Los Angeles

ISBN   1-882711-20-3

AQA Co.
155 S. El Molino Av.
Pasadena, CA 91101
Phn: (626) 796 9000
Fax: (626) 796 9070

Printed in the United States of America

To Ellie

Preface

ISO 14001 is making a big splash in corporate waters. This is because it forces companies everywhere to take a close look at how they manage their environmental activities and reduce risk. Although intended as a voluntary standard, governmental agencies, including the U.S. Department of Energy, the National Aeronautics and Space Administration, and the U.S. Department of Defense are considering ISO 14001 certification for their own use and as a requirement for their suppliers. Companies that fail to establish ISO 14001 management systems will soon find it difficult to compete in foreign markets. Thus, market forces, government mandates and the growing pressure of public groups urging companies to operate sound environmental practices will, ultimately, prod the universal adoption of ISO 14001.

External forces are not the only ones driving ISO 14001. Many companies also recognize the internal need for a sound environmental management system and have encouraged the creation of a common, internationally accepted, environmental management system standard. Hoping to thwart the duplicative, and often competitive nature of command-and-control legislation, corporate leaders are committed to ISO 14001 because it makes their companies more competitive in the global economy. Simply stated, companies that carry out ISO 14001 find that they waste fewer resources, reduce liabilities, improve their public image, and increase profits.

This book familiarizes its readers with some legal aspects of ISO 14001. The author does not intend it to be a legal treatise. Rather, it considers seven of the most troubling legal issues raised by ISO 14001 for U.S. organizations, registrars and auditors. It then identifies strategies for maximizing the benefits and reducing the pitfalls of each of these issues.

The strategies offered by the author are both legal and procedural. The legal strategies consist primarily of the strategic use of privilege, immunity and amnesty. Because legal strategies vary from state to state and situation to situation, this book explains them only in general terms. Only an attorney familiar with the facts and law of a particular situation can provide effective legal advice.

The more important strategies are procedural. They consist of good management practices that by their nature help the organization avoid unnecessary exposure to legal liability.

This book has five intended audiences: organizational top management; organizational implementers; regulators; auditors and registrars. For top management, it is a quick read, designed to provide a global overview of the legal pitfalls and benefits of the standard. Organizational implementers, including management's representative, will want to use this book as an implementation guide. Regulators, advocating environmental management systems, should use the book to develop a clearer understanding of organizational concerns involved in full disclosure and strict liability. Finally, auditors and registrars will find the book useful in designing audits that ensure conformance to ISO 14001 without creating unnecessary legal liability for themselves or the auditee.

The remainder of this book is divided into three sections. In Chapters 1 through 3, the book outlines the seven unique legal issues raised by ISO 14001. It then considers ISO 14001 and U.S. law and regulation. Finally, it provides a basic primer on the legal concepts necessary to understand ISO 14001's advantages and pitfalls.

Chapters 4 through 10 are an in-depth discussion of each of the seven unique legal issues raised by the standard. These chapters include strategies for maximizing the legal advantages and reducing the disadvantages.

Chapter 11 changes the focus from the organization to the individual. It considers the legal issues for specific organizational participants. Finally, Chapter 12 considers legal issues for registrars and auditors.

This book is one of a series published by AQA. The other books in the series are: *ISO 14001 Documentation*; *ISO 14001 Requirements*; and *ISO 14001 In Our Company*. Together, these books form a complete library for the environmental management systems professional. The series is annotated at the back of this book.

The author wishes to acknowledge the partners and staff of Higgs, Fletcher & Mack LLP who made this effort possible. Particular thanks to John Morrell, Charles V. Berwanger, Darlene Shelton-Mora and Romi Simons. Finally, heartfelt thanks to: Chris, Josh, Elsie, Joel, Annie, John and Bernie.

The author and publisher of this book wish you the best of luck in the implementation of ISO 14001 in your organization. ISO 14001 is a tool that will allow us to bring environmental management into the boardroom for the benefit of the organization, our children and the environment.

Contents

CHAPTER 4   INITIAL ENVIRONMENTAL REVIEW

CHAPTER 5   ENVIRONMENTAL POLICY

CHAPTER 8   SELF-EVALUATION OF COMPLIANCE

CHAPTER 9   ENVIRONMENTAL MANAGEMENT SYSTEM AUDITS

CHAPTER 10   MANAGEMENT REVIEW

CHAPTER 11   LEGAL ISSUES FOR ORGANIZATIONAL PARTICIPANTS

CHAPTER 12   LEGAL ISSUES FOR REGISTRARS
AND AUDITORS

APPENDIX

UNIQUE LEGAL ASPECTS OF ISO 14001

This chapter identifies and summarizes seven hotbutton legal issues in ISO 14001. These are not the only legal issues presented by the standard. However, they represent the most pressing concerns for organizations during the implementation phase. A whole chapter will be later dedicated to each issue. This chapter only introduces these issues and identifies their scope. These issues are:

- Initial environmental review;
- Development of the environmental policy;
- Identification of legal requirements and voluntary standards;
- Integration of emergency preparedness and response into the environmental management system;
- Self-evaluation of compliance;
- Environmental management systems audits; and
- Management review of the EMS.

Additionally, this chapter considers the relationship between ISO 14001 and ISO 14004. Although registrars limit their interpretation of ISO 14001 to sections three and four, courts may use all of ISO 14001 and 14004 as a basis for identifying an organization's obligations.

INITIAL ENVIRONMENTAL REVIEW

The initial environmental review is the process by which the organization identifies its environmental impacts and aspects. ISO 14001 Section 4 does not require the initial review; therefore, it is not an auditable component of the registration process. However, it is an obvious and essential element in developing policies, objectives and targets. The review also provides a baseline for measuring continual improvement through management review.

Both the ISO 14001 Annex and ISO 14004 suggest that part of the initial review should be a consideration of the organization's compliance with environmental rules, regulations and voluntary standards. This self-evaluative process can open the door to civil and criminal liability by identifying a prior regulatory noncompliance or a significant negative environmental impact.

ENVIRONMENTAL POLICY

ISO 14001 requires the organization to develop an environmental policy and make that policy available to the public. The policy must contain certain elements including commitments to compliance with environmental regulations and voluntary standards; prevention of pollution; and continuous improvement of the EMS. The Annex and ISO 14004 expand the idea of the policy to include issues identified in the initial environmental review.

The policy can become a broad-ranging statement and commitment by the organization's top management to comply with regulations and to improve it's environmental impacts and the EMS. Because the organization must make this document available to the public, the organization must assume that the public will rely upon it. Thus, the development of an environmental policy raises issues of misrepresentation by top management if the organization fails to fulfill the commitments stated in the policy.

IDENTIFICATION OF LEGAL REQUIREMENTS

ISO 14001 requires that a registered organization identify the legal requirements and voluntary standards to which it is subject. The Annex and ISO 14004 suggest the compilation of a list as a method to meet this requirement. However, because the drafters intended ISO 14001 as an international standard, neither the Annex nor ISO 14004 completely reflects the magnitude of this obligation under current U.S. command-and-control legislation.

Given the myriad of statutes, regulations, policies and voluntary standards that a U.S. organization may be subject to, the simple task of identifying which rules, regulations, statutes and standards apply to the organization is a monumental task. This raises several legal questions. First, how should an organization effectively approach this task. Second, what are the necessary qualifications of the person or persons charged with completing this task. Third, what is the potential liability for failure to identify all of the rules, regulations, voluntary standards and statutes to which the organization is subject.

EMERGENCY PREPAREDNESS AND RESPONSE

ISO 14001 requires an organization to establish and maintain procedures for responding to accidents and emergencies. The drafters amplify this element of the standard in ISO 14004. The organization should have adequate emergency plans and procedures for accidental emissions to the atmosphere, water, land and any other specific environmental or ecosystem impact that might result from an accidental release.

For industrial organizations already covered by the Emergency Planning and Community Right to Know Act (EPCRA), this element of the standard should not represent a new burden. In fact, the standard should help the organization assure that it is meeting its legal obligations under EPCRA. However, for those organizations not covered by EPCRA, ISO 14001 imposes new responsibilities to assure that the organization has planned for foreseeable emergencies. This obligation may also bring potential liabilities by identifying foreseeable emergencies for which the organization has failed to prepare or respond.

SELF-EVALUATION OF COMPLIANCE

ISO 14001 requires the organization to establish and maintain documented procedure for periodically evaluating compliance with relevant environmental legislation and regulations. This requirement implicates many of the same concerns raised by the initial environmental review and the identification of legal requirements and voluntary standards. However, unlike the initial environmental review, this element is specifically required, and is auditable, under the standard.

This element of the standard has significant implications for third-party auditors, registrars and the organization itself. If the standard requires organizations to self-audit for compliance, what are the professional standards of care required to conduct such audits? How will outside auditors and registrars evaluate the organization's identification of regulations and voluntary standards and determine the identification to be adequate? How will auditors and registrars evaluate compliance with identified regulations and voluntary standards? What must be documented and to what degree of specificity? What obligations do auditors and registrars have to reveal a noncompliance with identified requirements and voluntary standards?

ENVIRONMENTAL MANAGEMENT SYSTEM AUDITS

The environmental management system audit verifies that the organization has implemented, and maintained, the environmental management system and that the EMS itself is relevant and effective. The intended focus of the EMS audit is the environmental management system itself as an organizational tool. The intended audience for EMS audit results is the top management, who will consider them as part of the management review.

These internal self-audits are valuable to organizations committed to control, and continuous improvement, of the EMS. However, they raise civil liability issues. Environmental management system audits reveal weaknesses in the EMS that, if not corrected, a court could characterize as negligent. The organization must carefully consider how to conduct these audits to maintain their value as information gathering and assessment devices without creating undue liability exposure.

MANAGEMENT REVIEW

Management review is a key responsibility of top management. The purpose of management review is the evaluation of the suitability, adequacy and effectiveness of the EMS. At a minimum, these reviews must include consideration of internal audit results, changing circumstances, and the commitment to continual improvement.

The management review places top management in the liability spotlight. This documented assessment, if made public, can provide outside parties with evidence of top management's failure to respond to identified weaknesses in the EMS that, in turn, resulted in a regulatory noncompliance or a serious negative environmental impact. The reviews may also provide proof of top management's failure to provide sufficient resources to carry out the environmental policy. Such evidence can be proof of civil or criminal liability.

ISO 14001 APPENDIX AND ISO 14004

ISO 14001 Section 4 is the only element of the ISO 14000 series to which an organization can register. Thus, auditors and registrars frequently focus on this section of the standard to the exclusion of the Annex and ISO 14004. Registrars argue that since they can only register an organization to ISO 14001 Section 4 they must limit their examination of an organization's EMS to the elements defined therein.

American jurisprudence is more far-ranging in its views. Although courts would probably consider ISO 14001 Section 4 as the core of the standard, they will look to the Annex and ISO 14004 as persuasive supporting documents. This is analogous to the way courts decide questions of legislative interpretation. They will look to the legislation first. However, if that legislation is unclear, they will look to the legislative history and other supporting documents to fill in the gaps. Thus, from a legal perspective, the ISO 14001 Annex and ISO 14004 must be carefully considered in interpreting the standard.

NOTE

Focusing on legal issues, this book does not address all requirements of the standard. For in-depth interpretation of the whole standard please refer to *ISO 14001 REQUIREMENTS, 61 Requirements Checklist and Compliance Guide* book by Jack Kanholm. It is annotated in the catalog at the back of this book.

2 ISO 14001 IN THE U.S. REGULATORY ENVIRONMENT

This chapter discusses how ISO 14001 fits (and doesn't fit) in the current U.S. regulatory environment. It then considers how ISO 14001's role is likely to evolve. What specific legal advantages can an organization expect from carrying out ISO 14001? How does ISO 14001 help reduce legal risks through improved management? What are the legal downsides?

ENVIRONMENTAL MANAGEMENT SYSTEMS IN THE CURRENT REGULATORY ENVIRONMENT

The U.S. regulatory environment is changing. Those changes favor environmental management systems over alternative command-and-control regulatory models. Two of those drivers are cost and world trade.

Cost

The first, and most significant, driver for change in the environmental regulation is the popular demand that government reduce its size and cost. Command-and-control regulation is expensive. It requires armies of bureaucrats to develop thousands of regulations. Once created, those regulations require additional armies of inspectors to ensure the compliance of organizations. Finally, command-and-control regulation requires armies of administrative law judges and attorneys to make examples of organizations who fail to meet the letter of every regulation.

The costs of command-and-control systems are no longer socially tolerable. Given limited resources, governments and society must make choices. Do we want to spend more money on inspectors or educators, administrative law judges or Medicare, bureaucrats or tax relief. Environmental management systems represent an opportunity to reduce the cost of a high quality environment and to transfer many of the remaining costs to the private sector. With environmental management systems, organizations become responsible for regulating themselves, absorbing most of the costs.

World Trade

The second factor changing the current regulatory environment is the increased level of world trade. Like the cost of labor, a country's environmental regulatory scheme affects the cost of manufacture. In an open market system, environmental compliance costs must be competitive.

Traditional command-and-control regulation ignores the realities of this world economy and, therefore, is inherently isolationist. Command-and-control systems set standards in a vacuum. Alternatively internationally adopted environmental management systems such as ISO 14001, EMAS and the Dutch covenants recognize the realities of the new global economy allowing organizations from all nations to compete on a level playing field.

It is true that some organizations, in some countries, may use ISO 14001 as an excuse to continue to operate as environmental outlaws. However, those countries and organizations will rapidly become the minority rather than the majority because ISO 14001 provides a high level of visibility for bad actors.

Thus, at a time when both political parties are demanding downsizing of government and a commonsense approach to regulation, environmental management systems will continue in their ascendancy over traditional command-and-control models. Further, when organizations must compete in a world economy, societal standards as important as the environment must be measured using an international yardstick rather than operating in an isolationist, command-and-control vacuum.

THE TRANSITION FROM COMMAND-
AND-CONTROL TO SELF-REGULATION MODELS

The International Organization for Standardization developed ISO 14001 through an international consensus process. In many respects this process fails to recognize, or be sensitive to, the specific regulatory environment of each participating nation. This is particularly significant for countries such as the United States that have a long tradition of legislative regulation in the environmental arena.

Since the inception of the United States' environmental regulatory schemes during the 1970's, Congress, and the states, opted for a command-and-control model. In this model, legislatures and delegated agencies specified standards that organizations must meet for the disposal of wastes and emissions to the land, air and water.

At its inception, the command-and-control model was effective and efficient. It responded to this country's most egregious environmental problems by specifying emission standards and methods of achieving those standards.

However, during the last twenty-five years, as organizations' environmental perspective matured, the command-and-control model's cost effectiveness diminished. Organizations now realize that pollution prevention is synonymous with good management and higher profitability. Organizations now opt for pollution prevention strategies, reducing both emissions and the wasteful use of expensive raw materials and energy. Thus, the marketplace now drives improved environmental performance.

Today the inflexibility of the command-and-control model leaves organizations with little choice in responding to environmental impacts. The regulatory structures of command-and-control force organizations to invest huge sums of money in regulatory paperwork and end-of-pipe control. Unfortunately, those dollars often could be better spent in pollution prevention and product stewardship. The result is that greater and more stringent regulation leads only to smaller and more costly increments of environmental improvement.

The SEC Model

In contrast to the command-and-control model, the Securities and Exchange Acts of 1933 and 1934 created a full disclosure, self-regulation model. The underlying philosophy of these acts was that, in a full disclosure environment, the marketplace would regulate organizations by financially rewarding the responsible and penalizing the irresponsible. This full disclosure model is highly effective.

Publicly traded corporations routinely submit third-party audits to the Securities and Exchange Commission, the stock exchanges, and their stockholders. Because investors can rely on the information presented in those reports, the public becomes the ultimate arbiter of appropriate organizational behavior by bidding stock prices up or down. Thus, full disclosure leads to self-regulation.

The European Model

Outside the United States, other governments have moved toward full environmental disclosure models, such as European Eco-Management and Audit Scheme (EMAS). EMAS represents a compromise in which governments exchange disclosure for limited regulatory controls.

In March 1992, the European Union (EU) proposed a regulation to encourage businesses to review and improve their environmental performance continuously. The EU adopted this Eco-Management and Audit Scheme (EMAS) in 1993. EMAS officially went into effect on April 10, 1995.

Because it is an EU regulation, the EU requires that all member nations adopt it. EMAS applies to companies operating sites in Europe where an organization performs industrial activity. Although the notion of nonmandatory regulation is hard for Americans to accept, participation in EMAS by particular sites or companies is entirely voluntary. In fact, the EU is using EMAS as a test to see if organizations can achieve environmental improvement from market forces alone, without the kind of complex regulatory and enforcement system that we have in the United States.

To register to EMAS, a site has to meet the following criteria: 1) adopt an environmental policy that includes a commitment to continuous improvement of environmental performance; 2) conduct an environmental review of the site; 3) set up a program and an environmental management system to address the results of the review and to achieve the environmental policy; 4) conduct environmental audits at the site; 5) set specific objectives, based on audit results, and update the environmental program to meet those objectives; 6) prepare an environmental statement specific to the site; 7) have environmental policy, program, management system, review/audit procedure, and environmental statements examined by an independent, accredited environmental verifier to confirm that they meet the requirements of the regulation; 8) forward the validated environmental statement to the appropriate body of the member state in which the site is located for communication to the public, as appropriate, after registration.

Most EMAS requirements regarding environmental policy, environmental management system, conducting internal EMS audits, and having specific environmental objectives and a plan to meet them, are similar to the ISO 14001 requirements. In fact, the European Union has now accepted ISO 14001 as the equivalent of EMAS for non-EU organizations shipping goods into the EU.

Despite these similarities, however, EMAS and ISO 14001 have several critical differences. The origin and purpose of the two documents are quite different. EMAS is part of a regulation for the European Union and has the clearly stated purpose of improving the environmental performance of European industry. ISO 14001 is an international standard, developed to describe the core elements of an environmental management system.

EMAS focuses on the end result of improved environmental performance. ISO 14001 focuses on establishing an effective management system that should result in improved performance. This different focus explains why EMAS contains requirements for a policy that includes a commitment to performance improvements and a public environmental performance statement. The required public statement reports data describing and quantifying the company's environmental performance. An independent verifier must validate the statement.

LEGAL BENEFITS OF ISO 14001

The primary legal benefit of ISO 14001 is that it acts as a shield against legal risk. By certifying to the international standard, a company demonstrates its intent to comply with environmental regulations and societal norms. Companies that register to the standard may also experience significant regulatory and criminal protections.

Lender, Insurer, and Investor Liabilities

Lenders are subject to allegations of negligence, and their borrowers to allegations of misrepresentation, when they fail to consider environmental risks involved in making loans. As a result, financial institutions are becoming more sensitive to environmental risks and their impact on collateral. Third-party audited environmental management systems such as ISO 14001 protect both lenders and borrowers against suits by disgruntled stakeholders.

Insurance companies are fully aware of the risk to their policies created by poor environmental performance of the insured. Organizations with a sound and effective environmental management system can show that they pose less risk for the insurance company. This creates a negotiating tool for lower premiums and broader coverage.

Environmental responsibility has become a core value of the public, and that public includes investors. Institutional investors such as mutual funds and pension funds recognize the importance of environmental responsibility to the public. This is one driving force behind the SEC rule that investors have a right to know about significant environmental liabilities because these liabilities could have an impact on a company's overall performance. Thus, a sound environmental management system helps protect the corporation from allegations of investor fraud while increasing share values and access to capital markets.

Contractor and Supplier Liability

ISO 14001 requires that the organization establish procedures related to identified "significant" environmental aspects of operations and activities involving contractor services.

Organizations take extraordinary measures to identify contractors as independent entities, rather than employees or agents. However, the organization may still have significant liability exposure for a contractor's acts. ISO 14001 provides a way to reduce these liabilities. By requiring that contractors be ISO 14001 registered the company can first reduce the probability of an environmental impact. Further, if an accident occurs, the contractor's independent EMS may go far to limit claims of vicarious liability or negligent hiring.

Real Property Transactions

The ability to buy, sell and borrow against real property is essential to any fully functioning economy. Since the passage of CERCLA, many of these transactions have become fraught with danger, resulting in potential environmental liabilities. Environmental management systems increase the ability of an organization to divest itself of properties or to obtain credit based on the value of those properties. Having a history of environmental management system audits shows that the organization has identified and managed past liabilities and therefore provides greater assurance to prospective buyers and lenders. Further, early identification of environmental impacts allows the organization the time to correct problems before they erode real property values.

Securities and Exchange Commission

Concerns with the environment have captured the public's attention and environmental awareness is probably at an all-time high. This public interest has increased pressure on the Securities and Exchange Commission to ensure that publicly held companies are revealing in a fair, full and timely manner present and potential environmental costs of a material nature. Attorneys and accountants who follow the SEC expect the Commission's efforts to increase.

While some advocate that the SEC should attempt to enforce the security laws to effectively regulate corporate environmental conduct, the traditional SEC role of pressing for clear disclosure of all environmental information that is economically material to the registrant is more likely to be followed.

Stock values of corporations are sensitive to the annual financial report. Analysts believe that public response to corporate performance is closely tied to the organization's use of environmental management systems and environmental performance monitoring. This is leading toward a requirement that organizations reflect environmental management system audits in the corporate financial statement.

Identifying and interpreting environmental risk continues to be a challenge to the accounting industry. It is likely that certified public accountants will begin to rely on third-party audited systems such as ISO 14001 to provide the necessary analysis.

Regulatory and Criminal Liability

Industry, environmental groups and regulators are unifying around the theme that command-and-control systems have reached a plateau, isolating environmental efforts and failing to provide a holistic approach. Regulators in several states are moving to increase regulatory flexibility for organizations that set up an EMS, such as ISO 14001. Almost half the states have adopted laws granting some immunity to organizations that carrying out environmental-audit programs, report violations and take corrective action.

Right now, the regulatory requirements are the same for companies that adopt ISO 14001, but US EPA is actively discussing a two-tiered system. Mary McKiel, director of EPA's standards network, sees "regulators being transformed from punishing bosses to umpires that intervene only when something goes wrong."

Under this two-tiered approach, organizations who carry out third party audited environmental management systems would be subjected to fewer regulatory inspections and receive greater flexibility in their permits. Some EPA officials and many state legislatures have gone so far as to suggest that noncompliance discovered during regulatory audits could be corrected without a penalty by organizations who implement ISO 14001.

On the criminal front, the Department of Justice's policy for environmental criminal prosecutions encourages self-audits for environmental violations. DOJ's policy contains a "nondefinitive list" of factors that warrant lenient treatment of environmental law violators (see Appendix). Among those factors are the existence and scope of any "regular, intensive, and comprehensive environmental compliance program." An ISO 14001 environmental management system, with its related audit protocols, may qualify an organization for leniency.

Even more significant, perhaps, are the attitudes of state governments. For example, the Pennsylvania Department of Environmental Protection (DEP) issued a reformed audit policy under which DEP will not assess a civil penalty or pursue civil or criminal actions against a company that completes a compliance audit, reveals the problems uncovered in the audit to DEP, and takes action or sets a schedule to correct the violations (see Appendix).

Civil Liability

Imagine that your organization just had an environmental incident in which several neighbors are complaining of trouble breathing and burning eyes. Not only do you have the regulatory agencies to worry about, you may, and probably will, be the subject of a civil suit. If the norm in your industry is to have an EMS, it is very likely that the neighbors' attorney will argue that your company's failure to have set up the EMS was a direct, or at least contributing, cause of the accident. Thus, in industries where EMS's are common, the lack of an EMS can result in civil liability.

Trade Barriers

The ISO 14000 series establishes internationally recognized standards that will diminish barriers to trade. This is important for importers, exporters and multinational organizations. The standardized system makes it easier for multinational organizations to gauge their environmental performance and make useful comparisons of facilities in different countries.

Certification to ISO 14001 will help organizations compete in foreign markets. In some foreign markets, certification will be an absolute requirement. Within countries where domestic industries wholeheartedly adopt ISO 14001, market pressures will make it difficult for outside companies to compete without ISO 14001 certification.

Those firms that choose to be among the first to seek and obtain certification to ISO 14001 may enjoy a distinct competitive advantage, no matter their country of origin or operation. Any organization involved in global commerce needs to make its own strategic business decisions, but ISO 14001 certification is a key decision that needs to be carefully considered. European communities have readily adopted ISO 9000 quality management standards and have begun adoption of EMAS environmental standards.

U.S. organizations may be somewhat behind the curve, but ISO 14001 is a new standard. The technical committee only approved it in September 1996. Further, because of the intensive environmental regulatory climate within the United States, most U.S. companies are already addressing some, if not many, of the elements encompassed in ISO 14001.

Arthur D. Little surveyed executives at 115 large North American businesses. They found that 61% expected meeting ISO 14001 to bring "potential competitive advantage." In addition, 48% said that failure to board the bandwagon could form a "potential nontariff trade barrier" given their expectation that customers around the world will require it. Thus, ISO 14001 may result in the loss of a company's competitiveness and the emergence of barriers to trade where

26 ISO 14001 AND THE LAW

the organization does not adopt the standard. However, for those who adopt it, ISO 14001 could be an important shield against unfair trade practices while opening new markets.

LEGAL RISKS OF ISO 14001

While the adoption of ISO 14001 has significant legal benefits, it also has potential legal risks. We can classify these risks in three categories. The first is the risk of revealing past regulatory infractions. The second is the risk that the system will provide evidence of a breach of the duty of care to third parties. The third is the risk that the misuse of such systems will result in a misrepresentation.

Disclosure of Strict Liability Regulatory Infractions

Many command-and-control regulations contain a strict liability component. The breach of such regulations does not require intent or negligence to constitute a violation. Like running a red light, the officer does not need to prove the driver's intent. The act itself is enough.

Frequently, regulations compound this strict liability aspect imposing upon organizations a duty to disclose. In combination, these regulations result in an obligation to tell the regulating agency about infractions over which the organization may have had no control but for which they are civilly or criminally responsible.

Traditionally, organizations solved this dilemma through blind ignorance. They assumed that, under these conditions, what they do not know cannot hurt them. The opposite is true. What they do know can hurt them.

ISO 14001 prescribes an environmental and management system that its drafters intend to provide information on the organization's environmental posture to the highest levels of management. Management systems are usually considered valuable by senior management because they allow them to better manage the organization. Here, however, knowledge of the environmental management system's function and the organization's regulatory compliance posture may be just the information that senior management does not want to know about.

Liability Road Maps

ISO 14001 provides a method for assessing and managing environmental risks. It does so by considering the organization's environmental aspects and their impacts and then making policy and management decisions concerning which impact to prioritize. The organization then develops and funds objectives and targets to reduce negative environmental aspects it previously prioritized.

ISO 14001 requires the organization to document much of this information. Those documents may be discoverable in a toxic tort litigation. Thus, ISO 14001 provides a litigation road map for outside parties seeking to recover damages resulting from the organization's management decisions.

Misrepresentation

When an organization makes a public statement on which it intends, or should reasonably have known, that the public will rely, it runs the risk of liability for misrepresentation. ISO 14001 requires organizations and registrars to make certain information available to the public, including the organization policy statement and its registration status. If that policy or registration status does not fairly and accurately represent the current state of affairs and if others rely on those statements and are injured, the organization, and the registrar, may be liable.

SOME BASIC LEGAL CONCEPTS

To fully understand legal issues described in the remainder of this book, and to develop plans responding to those issues, it is necessary that the reader have a rudimentary understanding of the legal concepts involved. This chapter divides those concepts into five categories: legal risk, statutory law, tort law, procedural requirements and evidentiary standards.

LEGAL RISK

In evaluating the legal risks of ISO 14001, the reader must first understand the notion of legal risk. This book defines legal risk as the sum of three distinct components: actual damages, transactional costs and outrage.

Actual Damages

Actual damages are the type of risk that organizations most commonly predict. They are predicted by the probability of an injury times the magnitude of the injury's harm. Actual damages are generally the smallest component of legal risk. They are reflected by actual damages in a civil action and economic benefit penalties imposed by regulatory agencies.

Civil Damages

Courts intend the tort of negligence to compensate private parties for actual risk. Negligence consists of four elements: a duty; the breach of that duty; actual and proximate cause; and damages.

Each of us has a duty to act reasonably under the circumstances. However, some situations impose a heightened duty of care requiring that we go beyond what the reasonable person would do. Such situations include extremely hazardous activities such as the use of hazardous chemicals. Thus, in determining legal risk, the organization must first

cerning the discovery of a noncompliance through an environmental audit. Entitled "Incentives for Self-Policing Discovery, Correction and Prevention of Violations," the agency seeks to encourage self-auditing by offering a 100% reduction of gravity-based penalties when the applicant meets nine specific conditions. These conditions are as follows:

- Discovery of the violation through environmental audit or due diligence,

- Voluntary discovery and prompt disclosure,

- Discovery and disclosure independent of government or third-party plaintiffs,

- Prompt correction,

- Remediation,

- Measures taken to prevent recurrence,

- No repeat violations,

- Violation did not result in serious imminent or actual harm to human health or the environment, and

- Full cooperation with the agency.

Commentators point out that while the policy's nine conditions are daunting, unfortunately they are not sufficient to avoid substantial criminal and civil liability. First, the policy does not reduce economic benefit penalties. Thus, it creates the potential for extensive litigation about whether the organization incurred an economic benefit from the violation and, if so, how much. Second, the policy does not protect individuals. Officers, managers and employees remain subject to criminal prosecution from violations discovered through environmental audits. Finally, the organization's disclosure avoids a criminal referral only if the EPA concludes, after additional investigation, that management (1) was not consciously involved or willfully blind to the conduct in question or (2) did not otherwise conceal or condone the violations in "philosophy or practice." Thus, while federal policy protects the organization from some civil penalties, it leaves both the organization and its employees open to criminal charges and other civil liabilities.

4 INITIAL ENVIRONMENTAL REVIEW

While not strictly required by ISO 14001, most practitioners recognize that the initial environmental review is an essential element of the implementation plan. It provides objective data to identify the organization's environmental aspects, and associated impacts, and their significance.

The initial environmental review is not a gap analysis. A gap analysis identifies the components of the organization's existing environmental management system. It then evaluates the organization's current EMS for conformance to ISO 14001.

Should the organization choose to conduct an initial review, a word of caution is necessary. The initial environmental review includes an examination of the organization's compliance with applicable environmental laws and regulations. If the organization has not conducted periodic environmental compliance audits, the possibility exists that the initial review will uncover previously unknown noncompliances.

THE STANDARD

ISO 14001 does not mandate an initial environmental review. ISO 14004 Section 4.3.1 and ISO 14001 Annex A.3.1 strongly suggest the use of initial environmental reviews as a tool to give the organization the baseline information necessary to identify the organization's environmental aspects.

ISO 14001

Definitions

ISO 14001 does not define the term "initial environmental review."

14001

Section 4.3.1 requires "the organization shall establish and maintain procedure(s) to identify the environmental aspects of its activities, products or services that it can control and over which it can be expected to have an influence."

ISO 14001 Annex

Section A.3.1 explains Section 4.3.1. Section A.3.1 states, in part, that:

"Sub-clause 4.3.1 is intended to provide a process for an organization to identify significant environmental aspects that should be addressed as a priority by the organization's environmental management system. . . Information already developed for regulatory or other purposes may be used for this process. Organizations may also take into account the degree of practical control they may have over the environmental aspects being considered."

"An organization with no existing environmental management system should, initially, establish its current position with regard to the environment by means of a review. The aim should be to consider all environmental aspects of the organization as a basis for establishing the environmental management system."

"The review should cover four key areas:

- Legislative and regulatory requirements;
- Identification of significant environmental aspects;
- Examination of all existing environmental management practices and procedures;
- Evaluation of feedback from the investigation of previous incidents."

"The process to identify the significant environmental aspects associated with the activities at operating units should, where relevant, consider,

- emissions to air;
- releases to water;

- waste management;

- contaminated land;

- use of raw materials and natural resources;

- other local environmental and community issues."

ISO 14004

Section 4.1.3 defines the initial environmental review as "The current position of an organization with regard to the environment. The initial review can cover the following:

- Identification of legislative and regulatory requirements;

- Identification of environmental aspects of its activities, products or services so as to determine those that have or can have significant environmental impacts and liabilities;

- Evaluation of performance compared with relevant internal criteria, external standards, regulations, codes of practice and sets of principles and guidelines;

- Existing environmental management practices and procedures;

- Identification of existing policies and procedures dealing with procurement and contracting activities;

- Feedback from investigation of previous incidents of noncompliance;

- Opportunities for competitive advantage;

- The views of interested parties; and

- Functions or activities of other organization systems that can enable or impede environmental performance."

ISO 14004 also provides procedural recommendations for conducting the initial environmental review. "In all cases, consideration should be given to the full range of operating conditions, including possible incidents and emergency situations."

"The process and results of the initial environmental review should be documented and opportunities for EMS development should be identified."

ANALYSIS

ISO 14004 defines the term initial environmental review as "the current position of an organization with regard to the environment." ISO 14001 only requires that the organization establish and maintain a procedure to identify environmental aspects.

The Annex expands on ISO 14001 by declaring that the intent of Section 4.3.1 is to provide a process for an organization to identify significant environmental aspects. Further, the Annex states that organizations with no existing environmental management system should, initially, establish their current environmental position by means of a review.

The Annex and ISO 14004 identify several areas that the initial environmental review should cover. Four areas are common to both documents. They are:

- Identification of legislative and regulatory requirements;

- Identification of environmental aspects to decide those that have significant environmental impacts and liabilities;

- Examination of all existing environmental management practices and procedures; and

- An evaluation of responses from the investigations of previous incidents and noncompliance.

Finally ISO 14004 states that the organizations should document the process and results of the initial environmental review.

Read as a whole the intent of the drafters is clear. All organizations registering to the standard must establish and maintain a procedure for identifying their environmental aspects. Organizations with no existing EMS should conduct an initial environmental review. That review, at a minimum, should consider: identification of and compliance with legislative and regulatory requirements; existing environmental management practices; feedback from the investigation of previous incidents and noncompliance; and identification of environmental aspects. Finally, the organization should document the review.

THE LEGAL ASPECTS

The tendency of organizations to allow the initial environmental review to merge with an initial compliance audit or an initial gap analysis is almost unavoidable. ISO 14004 and the Annex require the organization to identify legislation and regulatory requirements and its existing environmental management practices. Considering these aspects without also considering the organization's civil and regulatory liabilities is difficult.

Specifically, the initial environmental review raises four legal concerns.

- First, the process may identify a prior regulatory noncompliance.
- Second, the process may identify failures to report a previously identified regulatory noncompliance.
- Third, the process requires that its conclusions be documented.
- Finally, the process requires a comprehensive review of the organization's environmental impacts.

Noncompliance

The standard is clear. The Annex requires organizations without an existing EMS to conduct an initial environmental review. One element of that review is the identification of legislative and regulatory requirements. ISO 14004 suggests that the initial environmental review evaluate the organization's compliance with relevant regulations. Thus, organizations without an EMS will probably include a compliance audit as part of their initial environmental review.

Compliance audits may lead to the discovery of two types of regulatory noncompliance. First, the organization may identify previously undiscovered violations of known regulations. Second, because the standard requires the organization to catalogue its regulatory obligations, the organization may identify violations of previously unknown regulations.

Duty to Disclose

ISO 14004 and the Annex require the organization's initial environmental review to consider feedback from investigations of prior noncompliances and incidents. Thus, the initial environmental review may reveal obligations of the organization to reveal prior regulatory infractions. As discussed in Chapter 3, the penalties for failure to report a regulatory noncompliance are frequently much harsher than the penalty for the noncompliance itself.

Negligence

As previously discussed in Chapter 3, the tort of negligence has four elements: a duty, a breach of that duty, causation, and harm. ISO 14004 suggests that the organization document the initial environmental review. By following this recommendation, the organization may be documenting discoverable evidence of negligence.

Duty

ISO 14004 suggests that the organization evaluate its performance compared with relevant internal criteria, external standards, regulations, codes of practice and sets of principles and guidelines. This activity acts to document a bundle of duties that the organization may owe to third parties.

Breach of Duty

The organization breaches its duty by violating a statute or regulation or by failing to meet its duty of care as described in Chapter 3. ISO 14004 asks the organization to consider in its initial environmental review feedback from investigation of previous incidents of noncompliance. The Annex requires that the organization evaluate feedback from the investigation of previous incidents. When the organization documents these evaluations, as ISO 14004 suggests, those documents may provide discoverable evidence of the breach of a duty.

Causation

Negligence requires the plaintiff to prove cause-in-fact and proximate cause. The Annex suggests that organizations consider: air emissions; releases to water; waste management; and contamination of land. These documented considerations can provide evidence of causation.

Nuisance and Trespass

The initial environmental review looks beyond the fence line. ISO 14004 suggests that the review include the views of interested parties. The Annex requires a review of emissions to land, air and water.

Nuisance is conduct that is a substantial and unreasonable interference with another's use and enjoyment of land. Thus, the review may provide the evidentiary basis for such a claim. If the review identifies an entry onto another's property, such as emissions into air or water that are deposited onto someone else's land, the organization may be liable for trespass.

LEGAL STRATEGIES

The goal of the initial environmental review is to objectively evaluate the organization's environmental aspects and impacts. However, in a strict liability, command-and-control environment, such a review may be an invitation to civil and criminal liability.

Three legal strategies are available to the implementation team to conduct a broad ranging initial environmental review without exposing the organization to legal liabilities. These are: privilege the information, or seek amnesty or immunity for information revealed.

Privilege

Three forms of privilege may be applicable for protecting the conclusions of the initial environmental review. The applicability of each of these strategies varies between jurisdictions and organizations. The implementation team should explore each option carefully with legal counsel.

Statutory Privilege

In some jurisdictions, the initial environmental review may be definitionally equivalent to an environmental audit and, therefore, privileged under that state's environmental audit privilege legislation. Implementation teams should carefully review existing state legislation and, where possible, attempt to shape the initial environmental review to qualify for the privilege.

Approximately half the states now provide statutory privileges for environmental audits. These statutes vary from one jurisdiction to the next. However, most appear to encompass the initial environmental review to the extent that the review touches on issues of noncompliance or the failure to report a noncompliance.

The implementation team should consult with legal counsel to decide whether the privilege exists in the organization's state. If so, the implantation team should consult legal counsel concerning the breadth of the privilege and any specific requirements concerning its use.

The implementation team also needs to consider carefully the applicability of any statutory privilege to federal agencies and private citizens. The federal government does not recognize, and is not bound by, such privileges. Further, state statutes vary broadly concerning their applicability to private litigation.

Self-Evaluatory Privilege

The self-evaluative privilege has limited value in protecting a noncompliance or the failure to report a noncompliance. However, it may protect information developed in the initial environmental review from private parties.

Because the self-evaluative privilege is a creature of the courts, its scope and application vary from one state to the next. The implementation team needs to carefully review the applicability of this doctrine with legal counsel.

The privilege may protect the initial environmental review from civil discovery. The review is an after-the-fact self-analysis of past environmental aspects and impacts. The organization conducted the review to help top management develop the organization's environmental policy. Therefore, top management allowed the review with the expectation of privacy. Because the review is not an auditable element of ISO 14001, the organization can assert its confidentiality against outside parties such as auditors or registrars. Finally, without the existence of the privilege, organizations would not conduct initial environmental reviews.

Attorney Client Privilege

The attorney client privilege has limited applicability in protecting the initial environmental review. If the implementation team chooses this strategy, top management should request a legal opinion from counsel.

If the organization requests that legal counsel conduct a review of its legally mandated environmental obligations, counsel can conduct an audit to detect compliance with those obligations. This procedure may privilege the attorney's legal conclusions concerning the compliance audit aspects of the initial environmental review.

However, the organization may not use the privilege for a criminal or tortuous purpose. Thus if the organization has a duty to reveal a noncompliance, the attorney client privilege will not abrogate that responsibility.

This application of the attorney client privilege is difficult to sustain. Most courts require that the communication be in anticipation of litigation and for the purpose of rendering a legal opinion. Thus, the organization, if challenged, will have the burden of proving that they conducted the compliance audit component of the initial environmental review in anticipation of litigation and to obtain a legal, rather than a business, opinion.

Finally, the organization waives the privilege by broad distribution of the information. Therefore, the implementation team must be very careful to share its findings only with legal counsel. This may defeat the entire purpose of the initial environmental review.

Amnesty and Immunity

Many states now provide immunity to organizations that discover and promptly correct an environmental noncompliance. Even, the federal government has a policy of reducing the legal consequences for prompt correction of a noncompliance discovered during an initial environmental review. While these protections are not absolute, the implementation team should review this strategy with counsel.

PROCEDURAL STRATEGIES

The organization can tailor the initial environmental review's development to minimize legal risk. Procedurally, the organization can control the process to allow it to abort if necessary. The organization can design the end product to eradicate legally embarrassing documents.

The Process

Because the initial environmental review is not a required component of ISO 14001, the implementation team should carefully consider the development of procedural controls. One alternative is to design the audit in two phases. The first phase is a broad-based, general survey that focuses on understanding the environmental requirements and actual operating practices of the organization. The implementation team develops a general checklist designed to record relevant environmental aspects and impacts. The implementation team conducts this phase contemporaneously with the identification of legal regiments discussed in Chapter 6 under the direction of legal counsel.

From the information developed during the first phase, and the analysis of legal counsel, top management makes a judgment about the organization's potential environmental and legal liabilities. This subjective evaluation allows top management to decide whether the organization is ready to continue to phase two, or whether the potential exists for significant regulatory noncompliance and environmental impacts.

If top management decides that the organization is not yet ready to go on, the organization should immediately engage in a corrective action program designed to reduce legal risks under the direction of counsel. Once top management and counsel are satisfied that the organization has mitigated the risks to an acceptable level, the organization can continue to phase two.

In phase two, the organization subjects itself to a detailed compliance and environmental impact analysis. The analysis is tailored to the identification of significant environmental impacts, the development of solutions to mitigate those impacts and development of a regulatory compliance system. This approach allows organization to focus on reducing its legal liabilities before focusing in on issues of continuous improvement through pollution prevention and regulatory compliance.

The Product

The drafters of ISO 14001 and 14004 intended the initial environmental review solely to give the organization a description of significant environmental aspects and impacts. Thus, the end product should be a short report consisting of information that will not create legal risks.

The report should generally describe the organization's facility, including such regulated aspects as underground storage tanks, water treatment plants, incinerators, etc. It should describe the neighboring land uses and identify sensitive neighbors, such as residential areas, schools, wildlife habitats and water courses. It should generally describe the products or services produced and the raw materials used, especially to the extent that those raw materials or products contain EPCRA identified compounds. It should include a summary of the organization's EPCRA toxic release inventory, if such a report exists. The document should include a discussion of any past reported incidents or accidents.

The team should consider the following questions during the creation of the report. Is this a document the implementation team, or top management, would mind seeing in the *Wall Street Journal* or *Business Week*? Is this a document that the implementation team would ask the company's president to sign? Is this a document that the implementation team would be willing to discuss at a deposition or before a government agency, grand jury or trial jury? Is this a document that the implementation team, top management or shareholders would mind falling into the hands of a competitor or a plaintiff's attorney? Is this a document that the implementation team would wish to receive? If the answer to any of these questions is no, the team should give serious thought to redrafting the document or destroying it. A quick trip to the shredder could be the wisest decision.

In developing any written documents during the initial environmental review, the implementation team should follow some simple rules:

- Let the document sit overnight; set it aside for review in the morning. Then the team should ask the same set of questions listed above, making appropriate modifications.

- Make certain that the team limits the scope and focus of any document to what is appropriate. Remove any unsolicited opinions, asides, personal attacks or comments.

- Have someone else review it. Ask a trusted colleague, not on the implementation team, to review the communication. Have that person try to read it through the eyes of an attorney.

- Use the organization's letterhead sparingly. Because documents printed on a company letterhead can have greater legal impact and authority, the team should produce and circulate such documents with special care.

- Destroy the paper trail. Save only necessary and valuable documents. Dispose of all hard copy drafts in the shredder. Treat flip charts and photographic white boards like any other written draft.

- Remember e-mail. Apply these rules to all your communications despite how fleeting or innocent the medium. Misdirected or recovered e-mail can figure prominently in environmental cases. Send it with care and erase files. Be aware that an intrepid investigator may still retrieve deleted electronic data from backup or storage devices.

- Hold the carbon copies. Distribute E-mail, faxes, photocopies or documents only to essential recipients. Limiting circulation is especially important because forwarding these transmissions to others is so easy.

- Follow the rules. Know, understand and strictly comply with your company's documentation retention policies. Make sure that corporate counsel reviews these rules.

- Talk it out. Implementation team members can avoid much of the legal danger inherent in the initial environmental review simply by speaking up. Direct oral communications are still quick, safe and reasonably secure.

For further discussion of related issues please refer to *ISO 14001 REQUIREMENTS, 61 Requirements Checklist and Compliance Guide* book by Jack Kanholm (annotated in the catalog at the back of this book).

ENVIRONMENTAL POLICY

The environmental policy must originate from the organization's top management. Development of the policy is the step that galvanizes the organization and focuses it on addressing its environmental aspects and impacts. The policy summarizes how the organization plans to meet the requirements of ISO 14001.

THE STANDARD

The environmental policy is the core element of ISO 14001. It defines the overall environmental principles of the organization.

Because of the central role played by the environmental policy in the development and maintenance of the environmental management system, the drafters carefully defined what they meant by an adequate environmental policy. ISO 14001 and 14004 both define the term "environmental policy." ISO 14001, the Annex and 14004 carefully describe and explicate the term.

ISO 14001

Definitions

Section 3.9 defines environmental policy as a "statement by the organization of its intentions and principles in relation to its overall environmental performance which provides a framework for action and for the setting of its environmental objectives and targets."

14001

The standard requires that "top management shall define the organization's environmental policy to ensure that it:

- Is appropriate to the nature, scale and environmental impact of its activities, products or services;
- Includes a commitment to continual improvement and prevention of pollution;
- Includes a commitment to comply with relevant environmental legislation and regulations, and with other requirements to which the organization subscribes;
- Provides the framework for setting and reviewing environmental objectives and targets;
- Is documented, implemented and maintained and communicated to all employees;
- Is available to the public."

ISO 14001 Annex

"The environmental policy is the driver for implementing and improving the organization's environmental management system so that it can maintain and potentially improve its environmental performance. The policy should therefore reflect the commitment of top management to compliance with applicable laws and continual improvement. The policy should be sufficiently clear to be capable of being understood by internal and external interested parties and should be periodically reviewed and revised to reflect changing conditions and information."

"The organization's top management should define and document its environmental policy within the context of the environmental policy of any broader corporate body of which it is a part and with the endorsement of that body, if there is one."

ISO 14004

ISO 14004 defines environmental policy as a "statement by the organization of its intentions and principles in relation to its overall environmental performance which provides a framework for action and for setting of its environmental objectives and targets."

Section 4.1.4 then provides a rationale for establishing a policy and a list of elements and issues that the policy should address.

"An environmental policy establishes an overall sense of direction and sets the principles of action for an organization. It sets the goal as to the level of environmental responsibility and performance required of the organization, against which all subsequent actions will be judged. . .

The responsibility for setting environmental policy normally rests with the organization's top management. The organization's management is responsible for implementing the policy and for providing input to the formulation and modification of the policy.

An environmental policy should consider the following:

- The organization's mission, vision, core values and beliefs;
- Requirements of and communication with interested parties;
- Continual improvement;
- Prevention of pollution;
- Guiding principles;
- Coordination with other organizational policies (e.g. quality, occupational health and safety);
- Specific local and regional conditions;
- Compliance with relevant environmental regulations, laws and other criteria to which the origination subscribes."

ANALYSIS

Because the environmental policy is central to the development of an effective EMS, the implementation team must carefully review ISO 14001 and 14004 for answers to the following questions. What did the drafters mean by the phrase "environmental policy?" What are the essential elements of an adequate policy? Who is responsible for the environmental policy? Who is the intended audience for the environmental policy?

What is an Environmental Policy?

The drafters of ISO 14001 and 14004 developed two similar, but not identical, definitions of environmental policy. However, by reading definitions in context with the documents, an environmental policy as defined by ISO 14001 Section 3.9 and ISO 14004 consists of two distinct elements. These are:

- A statement of the organization's overall commitment to its environmental intentions and principles.

- A framework for achieving those intentions and principles.

Thus, a definitionally adequate environmental policy must identify the organization's commitments to the environment, and how it intends to achieve those commitments.

What are the Essential Elements of the Policy?

The definitions leave open the scope of specific commitments to environmental performance made by the organization and their achievement. However, ISO 14001 and 14004 identify a limited set of specific commitments and procedural elements that must be present in the policy. The required commitment elements are:

- A commitment to continual improvement;

- A commitment to prevention of pollution; and

- A commitment to comply with relevant environmental legislation, regulations and voluntary standards to which the organization subscribes.

The required procedural elements are:

- A framework that ensures the policy reflects the organization's internal culture including the organization's nature, scale, activities, products or services, mission, vision, core values, beliefs and principles.

- A framework that ensures the policy reflects the organization's external environment including specific local and regional conditions.

- A framework for coordinating the organization's environmental policy with other organizational policies and environmental policies of other organizations to which the registering organization is subordinate.

- A framework for setting and reviewing environmental objectives and targets.

- A framework for documenting, carrying out and communicating the policy.

Who is Responsible for the Policy?

The drafters were clear. "Top management shall define the organization's environmental policy." The policy, therefore, reflects the commitment of top management to the organization's environmental performance.

The drafters also clearly defined who they meant by top management. Top management is the individual, or group of individuals, with executive responsibility for the organization.

Who is the Intended Audience?

The drafters did not intend that the environmental policy become a dead letter. ISO 14001 requires that the organization communicate the policy to all employees and make it available to the public. The Annex and ISO 14004 state that the policy must be sufficiently clear that all internal and external interested parties can understand it.

THE LEGAL ASPECTS

The development of an environmental policy raises two legal concerns. First, if not properly written or carried out, the policy may be a misrepresentation for which the organization, and its top management, may be liable. Second, the policy is evidence of the organization's duty of care. A plaintiff's counsel may use it to support a claim of negligence.

Misrepresentation

The creation of an environmental policy has the potential to lead to allegations of misrepresentation. Its mere existence is evidence of three of the five elements of the tort.

The drafters intended that the policy be a factual statement concerning the organization's level of environmental responsibility and performance. In fact, ISO 14001 requires that the policy contain specific commitments concerning compliance, prevention of pollution and continual improvement. Thus, the organization, through its policy, makes a representation that it is committed to prevention of pollution and regulatory compliance.

The drafters require that the organization communicate the policy to employees and make it available to interested parties. This implies that the drafters intended interested parties to rely on the organization's policy statement.

Because the organization's policy statement is part of an internationally recognized environmental management system, reliance by interested parties appears reasonable. When the organization engages a third-party auditor to register it to ISO 14001, it heightens the reasonableness of this reliance.

Thus, if any of the representations in the policy turn out to be false and an interested party suffers an injury resulting from its reliance on the policy, the organization and its top management may be liable for misrepresentation.

Negligence

As discussed previously, the tort of negligence has four elements. The defendant owed the plaintiff a duty. The defendant breached that duty. The defendant's breach of duty was the actual and proximate cause of the plaintiff's harm. The plaintiff suffered a cognizable harm.

The creation of an environmental policy is proof of a duty. At a minimum, ISO 14001 requires that the policy include a commitment to compliance, prevention of pollution and continuous improvement. Plaintiff's counsel will read these commitments as identifiable duties.

If the plaintiff proves that the defendant failed to meet the duty and was harmed as a result, the plaintiff can recover his or her damages.

STRATEGIES AND RECOMMENDATIONS

In developing the policy the implementation team has four strategies at its disposal to reduce legal risks. First, the team needs to carefully scope the policy to ensure that it meets the content requirement of the standard and reflects the goals and aspirations of the organization without becoming a legal straightjacket. Second, the team must develop the policy so that it meets the procedural requirements outlined in ISO 14001 and 14004 but includes legal review and protections. Third, the team must work with senior management to develop appropriate strategies for making the policy available to interested parties without creating expansive classes of potential plaintiffs. Finally, the implementation team must plan for review of and revisions to the policy.

Scoping the Policy

How expansive should the policy be? At a minimum the implementation team must include statements concerning a commitment to comply, a commitment to prevent pollution and a commitment to continual improvement. Still, what else should the policy say?

The answer lies in the procedural elements for the development of the policy outlined in ISO 14001 and ISO 14004 discussed below. However, the implantation team must always remember that the policy is a public document on which the organization must stand or fall.

In crafting the environmental policy the implementation team needs to carefully consider both the developmental process and its choice of words. Here the implementation team faces a dilemma. The policy needs to be explicit enough to identify the organization's vision. However, if the policy becomes too specific, plaintiffs may use it to prove a misrepresentation by the organization, or the organization's failure to meet a defined duty of care. Thus, the policy statement needs to be aspirational rather than making binding commitments.

66 ISO 14001 AND THE LAW

Creating the Policy

The implementation team needs to focus on the policy as the core of their environmental management system. The policy should be both flexible and durable. It should allow the organization some "wiggle room" if it fails to achieve every goal, objective and target. It should not be so detailed that top management needs to revise it every month.

Words such as "will" or "shall" should always be combined with effort verbs such as "attempt" or "try." Remember that the heart of any environmental policy statement is a commitment to continual improvement, not an assertion that the organization will achieve specific goals or objectives.

In developing the policy, the implementation team should look at existing environmental policies adopted by the organization or the organization's parent. This will help the team in assuring itself that it has correctly identified top management.

The individual or group that ultimately approves the policy must have executive responsibility for the organization. If the parent organization has not delegated sufficient authority over environmental affairs to the subordinate organization's top management then the team will either seek a modification in the parent's policy or seek approval of the policy at a higher organizational level.

The implementation team may also wish to collect the environmental policy statements of other organizations. The team should give special attention to the policies of organizations accredited by the organization's preferred or selected registrar. Using these policies as models, the implementation team should fashion a preliminary policy statement that: meets the criteria of the standard; is in harmony with other policies approved by their registrar; and speaks to the specifics of the organization.

ISO 14001 and 14004 place the burden of policy approval on top management. However, this document must have the support of the entire organization. Therefore, the organization should review the policy at each management level prior to adoption. Legal counsel should review the final draft. Management should fully support what the policy says. Counsel must fully support how the policy says it.

Making the Policy Available

Making the policy available to the public raises additional legal issues for the implementation team. First, in making the document available to the public, how aggressively should the organization distribute it? Second, how should the organization notify the public of changes to its environmental policy?

The initial instinct of the implementation team is to take their newly approved policy and broadcast it extensively. The organization and the team are rightfully proud of this document. It represents a significant self-evaluation and consensus-building effort. However, the implementation team should temper this instinct with a certain degree of caution. Remember that the more aggressively the organization distributes its policy, the greater the number of interested parties entitled to rely upon it. Each interested party may, at some time in the future, have a cause of action for misrepresentation or negligence.

The best advice is to balance distribution against the policy's level of commitment. The more the policy commands the organization to meet specified goals, the more cautious the implementation team should be in its recommendations to top management concerning the policy's distribution. Conversely, if the implementation team carefully crafts the policy as an aspirational statement, the organization should feel free to publish it to the world.

Revising the Policy

Section 4.6 of ISO 14001 discusses the organization's obligation to review its environmental management system regularly. Chapter 10 more fully discusses legal aspects of management review. Because of the intimate relationship between policy review and policy development, we discuss this aspect of management review here.

The management review gives the organization an opportunity to reconsider commitments that it has been unable to fully carry out. If the organization initially insisted on absolute performance statements as part of its policy, and if the organization has been unable to achieve those absolute performances, the review provides an opportunity to either remove such statements from the policy entirely or convert them into more aspiration goals.

Generally, the better strategy is to modify absolute statements into aspirational ones. This allows the organization to continue to commit to achieving certain goals without misrepresenting its ability to do so.

As an example, an organization may state that it would comply with all storm water permit regulations. However, those regulations are nebulous at best. Upon review, the organization finds that it was unable to meet this absolute goal. Rather than completely abandoning the goal, the organization may change the statement to an aspiration such as, "the organization will attempt to achieve compliance with all storm water permit requirements."

As with the original policy statement, the organization must make the modifications available to the public. The organization should make modifications available in the same manner as the original policy. If the organization chose to make its original policy available through publication of a full page ad in the *New York Times*, it should use the same method for communicating each policy revision.

This prevents assertions by third parties that they did not know about policy changes and therefore relied on older versions. Expanding the methods by which modifications to the policy are distributed to the public is always acceptable. Contracting the availability of policy modifications is not advisable.

Requirements pertaining to the environmental policy are further discussed in *ISO 14001 REQUIREMENTS, 61 Requirements Checklist and Compliance Guide* book by Jack Kanholm (annotated in the catalog at the back of this book).

6 IDENTIFICATION OF LEGAL REQUIREMENTS

The benefits of a thorough identification of legal requirements and voluntary standards are obvious. It reduces the risk of a regulatory noncompliance or a civil liability while, in theory, reducing the organization's impacts on the environment. As with driving a car, knowing the rules of the road are a necessary condition precedent to complying with those rules and driving safely. Like traffic regulations, most environmental regulations have a strict liability component. Failure to have knowledge of the rules is no excuse for noncompliance.

While ignorance of the law is no excuse, many environmental regulations are a double-edged sword. First, the organization has a duty to comply with the regulations. Second, the organization may have a duty to reveal a noncompliance to the regulatory agency. Thus, the organization may be guilty of the infraction and guilty of failure to self-incriminate. An overarching understanding of the regulations may exacerbate the second duty of self-incrimination.

THE STANDARD

ISO 14001 does not intend to increase or change an organization's legal obligations. It requires that an organization establish and maintain a procedure to identify and have access to legal and other requirements to which the organization subscribes. This requirement should focus the organization on compliance with those laws and requirements.

ISO 14004 suggests that the organizations also understand and communicate its legal and voluntary obligations to employees. This requirement heightens the organization's, and its top management's, ability to comply with regulatory requirements.

ISO 14001

Definitions

ISO 14001 does not define legal and voluntary standards.

14001

Section 4.3.2 provides that "The organization shall establish and maintain a procedure to identify and have access to legal and other requirements to which the organization subscribes, that are applicable to the environmental aspects of its activities, products or services."

ISO 14001 Annex

Section A.3.2 provides examples of other requirements to which the organization may subscribe. These are:

- Industry codes of practice;
- Agreements with public authorities;
- Non-regulatory guidelines.

ISO 14004

Section 4.2.3 provides that "The organization should establish and maintain procedures to identify, have access to, and understand all legal and other requirements to which it subscribes, directly attributable to the environmental aspects of its activities, products, or services."

The section then provides some illustrative legal and other requirements for the organization's consideration.

- "How does the organization access and identify relevant legal and other requirements?
- How does the organization keep track of legal and other requirements?

- How does the organization keep track of changes to legal and other requirements?

- How does the organization communicate relevant information on legal and other requirements to employees?"

Finally, the section provides some practical help. "To maintain regulatory compliance, an organization should identify and understand regulatory requirements applicable to its activities, products or services. Regulations can exist in several forms:

- Those specific to the activity (for example, site operating permits):

- Those specific to the organization's products or services;

- Those specific to the organization's industry;

- General environmental laws;

- Authorizations, licensees and permits."

"Several sources can be used to identify environmental regulations and ongoing changes, including:

- All levels of government;

- Industry associations or groups;

- Commercial databases;

- Professional services."

"To facilitate keeping track of legal requirements, an organization can establish and maintain a list of all laws and regulations pertaining to its activities, products or services."

ANALYSIS

ISO 14001 and 14004 impose three distinct obligations on the organization.

- The organization must establish and maintain a procedure to identify the environmental laws and voluntary standards to which it is obligated.

- The organization must establish and maintain a procedure to assure access to current versions of environmental laws and voluntary standards to which it is obligated.

■ The organization must establish and maintain a procedure for understanding and communicating the laws and
voluntary standards to which it is obligated.

Identification

ISO 14001 Section 4.3.2 requires that "The organization
shall establish and maintain a procedure to identify . . .
legal and other requirements to which the organization subscribes, that are applicable to the environmental aspects
of its activities, products or services." The Annex defines
"other requirements" as: industry codes of practice; agreements with public authorities; and non-regulatory guidelines. ISO 14004 provides a nonexclusive list of regulatory
requirements including: regulations specific to the organization's activity such as operating permits; regulations specific to the organization's products or services; regulations
specific to the organization's industry; general environmental laws; and authorizations, licenses and permits.

The scope of environmental rules, regulations and standards is breathtaking. Federal government, state government, subdivisions of the state and traditional common law
create complex, contradictory and overlapping regulatory
schemes. Additionally, the organization, through its participation in various trade organizations, may subscribe to
a panoply of additional standards. Failure to appropriately identify each regulatory requirement or voluntary standard to which the organization subscribes can lead to significant negative legal consequences.

Many environmental statutes and regulations are geograph-
ically specific. Laws change from one state to another. Air
quality requirements vary from attainment to non-attain-
ment districts. Organizations with multiple facilities need to
identify and have access to the laws and regulations applicable to each geographic location. This issue also arises for organizations moving from one geographic location to another.

Within the same geographic location and during the same
time the rules and regulations that impact organizations will
vary based on the size and complexity of the organization.

Organizations should conduct facility specific reviews to assure that the regulatory scope is appropriate to the specific organization.

ISO 14004 requires that the organization keep track of changes in legal and other requirements. Statutes and voluntary commitments change over time. Reviewing those obligations as part of an ISO 14001 EMS is essential. Some critics of environmental management systems have suggested that the cost for small- and medium-sized enterprises (SME's) of conducting these routine surveys are too burdensome. However, by acting collectively through trade associations or other work groups, SME's can meet this requirement.

Access

ISO 14001 Section 4.3.2 requires that "The organization shall establish and maintain a procedure to . . . have access to legal and other requirements to which the organization subscribes, that are applicable to the environmental aspects of its activities, products or services." ISO 14004 suggests that the organization demonstrate access by establishing and maintaining a list of all laws and regulations concerning the organization's activities, products or services. However, the creation of a list, even an updated one, is not enough.

If an organization is to understand and communicate its regulatory obligations and voluntary commitments to its employees, it must first have access to copies of the obligations and commitments, to read and understand them. The idea that a simple list of statutes suffices trivializes the standard. A list of obligations is documented evidence that the organization identified its regulatory and voluntary standards. It is not evidence that the organization understood or communicated those obligations to employees.

Knowledge

ISO 14001 is silent on the organization's obligation to understand and communicate legal and other requirements to which to the organization subscribes. However, ISO 14004 makes clear that the organization must also understand these obligations and communicate them to employees.

ISO 14001 is the product of an international consensus. It does not identify the specific qualifications of the individuals charged with the responsibility for interpreting the organization's legal obligations and communicating those obligations to employees. This results in substantial debate within the US environmental community concerning who qualifies to handle this responsibility. The fact is that the identification, interpretation and communication of environmental regulations and voluntary obligations require the skills of a multidisciplinary team of environmental attorneys and professionals.

Interpreting the statutes are not enough. ISO 14004 requires that organizations communicate their legal and voluntary commitments. This distribution of knowledge is a two-edged sword. Knowledge of the obligation increases the probability that employees will follow the law. However, knowledge may also bring a duty to reveal a noncompliance.

THE LEGAL ASPECTS

By identifying, interpreting and communicating the organization's legal requirements and voluntary obligations, ISO 14001 exposes the organization to three forms of legal liability. These are: misrepresentation, negligence per se, and regulatory noncompliance.

Misrepresentation

An organization registering to ISO 14001 represents to the world that it identified and has access to legal and other requirements to which it subscribes. When read with ISO 14004 the representation expands to understanding and communicating these obligations to employees. If that representation is false, legal liability may follow.

Suppose an insurance company issues an environmental liability policy relying on the organization's ISO 14001 registration as a statement that it had identified, understood and communicated to its employees its regulatory requirements. Suppose further that the insurance company pays out a claim resulting from an injury directly attributable to the organization's failure to comply with an environmental regulation that the organization failed to identify, understand or communicate. The insurance company can probably recover its losses from the organization, arguing that organization misrepresented an important fact on which the insurance company relied when it entered into the insurance contract.

If the misrepresentation was intentional or reckless the plaintiff may also recover punitive damages. Thus, in the example above, if the organization lied about its conformance with ISO 14001, or if it conducted its legal review, or the communication of that review, recklessly the insurance carrier may recover both its actual losses and punitive damages.

Noncompliance

Ignorance of the law is generally no excuse. However, as more organizations register to ISO 14001 regulators may begin to associate ignorance with an intent to violate the law. Where environmental agencies identify a regulatory noncompliance in an organization without an EMS, they may be more likely to refer for criminal prosecution.

Organizations who carefully examine their regulatory duties through a disciplined evaluation of the environmental laws may still face civil liability for the noncompliance of undiscovered obligations. However, it is much less likely that such oversights would lead to referrals for criminal prosecution under EPA's audit policy (see Appendix).

Negligence per se

As discussed in Chapter 3, negligence is the breach of a duty of care that was the actual and proximate cause of the plaintiff's injury. One way of proving the duty and breach elements of negligence is through the doctrine of negligence per se. If the defendant violates a statute or regulation and the plaintiff's injury was the type that the statute or regulation intended to protect against, then the defendant is negligent per se. The plaintiff needs only prove causation and damage to recover.

By creating an itemized list of environmental statutes to which the organization is obligated, the organization makes the claim of negligence per se easier to prove. The plaintiff will request the list of regulations identified by the organization. Armed with the list, the plaintiff needs only review them to find a violation that in some way relates to his or her harm. Once the organization creates the list, denying the regulation's applicability will be difficult.

STRATEGIES AND RECOMMENDATIONS

Like many other legal issues raised by ISO 14001, the best strategy when identifying legal requirements is to do it right. The implementation team must ensure that the scope and frequency of review are sufficient to reduce legal risk to acceptable levels. Top management must decide how much professional assistance the organization can afford and how much legal risk the organization is willing to accept when interpreting and communicating legal requirements and voluntary standards.

Scope of Review

The implementation team's first task is to identify the universe of applicable regulations. The team should begin this task by soliciting information from outside sources such as trade associations or other organizations to which the organization belongs. If those organizations have not yet identified the universe of environmental regulations obligating its members, the team should encourage them to do so.

When outside support is unavailable, and to confirm the accuracy of the information provided through outside sources, the team should employ an internal multi-tiered approach. The team can identify the applicable regulations and standards by sorting first by significant impact, then by media, then by jurisdiction and finally by voluntary standard.

The implementation team will have identified the organization's significant environmental impacts as part of the initial environmental review. This information then is grouped by the medium affected — land, air or water.

Legislatures tend to create environmental regulatory schemes by media. The team can then sort through all applicable statutes, rules and regulations by media and identify regulations applicable to the organization's impacts. As the implementation team sorts through the regulations and standards, it should keep a lookout for additional impacts it might have missed in its original analysis.

Because the federal delegation model allows states to regulate environmental aspects with a greater scope and a higher level of protection, it is generally advisable to start with the federal standards and then look to state, or local, regulations to see if they impose any additional obligations.

Finally, for each impact, the organization needs to review the manifestos of any voluntary organization to which it belongs. These manifestos may set a higher standard of care than regulatory agencies and, therefore, will set the compliance criteria.

There is no easy or simple way to go about this identification process. Information supplied by trade associations or other sources is helpful but probably not definitive. Trade associations may not take into account local standards or the voluntary standards of other organizations to which the organization belongs. However, several strategies are available to the implementation team to reduce the costs of this identification process.

First, share the load. If your trade association has not identified regulatory obligations for its industry, form a committee to do so. If you do not belong to a trade association, become involved. If there is no trade association for your organization, form one or, at a minimum, form some informal alliances with other companies who are organizationally similar.

Internally, identify personnel and documents that may have covered all or part of this ground in the past. Seek out prior compliance audits if they exist. Seek out environmental staff who may have already dealt with some of these issues. Look to corporate counsel. Any or all these sources may be a treasure trove of information. However, make sure that the implementation team's collection and use of these documents does not waive any preexisting privilege.

Second, plan ahead. Allow plenty of time. For most organizations, this is not a simple process. It requires substantial amounts of time and resources to conduct a thorough search.

Frequency of Review

Assembling the basic collection of regulatory and voluntary standards is just the beginning. The organization must routinely review those standards to assure conformity with changes in the organization and its environment.

Organizations change their activities and processes over time. This may change the organization's environmental impacts. As those impacts change, a review of regulatory and voluntary standards is necessary.

External to the organization, environmental regulations and voluntary standards change. Even if the organization continues to produce the same products in the same way with the same environmental impacts year after year, the regulatory scheme to which the organization is accountable changes. Thus, regular and routine reviews to identify new or changed regulations must also take place.

These ongoing reviews are neither as lengthy nor as expensive as the creation of the original compendium. However, they are equally important. The implementation team should build them into the EMS management review process.

Qualifications of the Reviewer

Section 4.3.2 of ISO 14001 requires that a registered organization identify and have access to applicable legislative, regulatory and other voluntary requirements to which the organization subscribes. However, because an international consensus created ISO 14001, it does not identify the specific qualifications of the individuals charged with this responsibility. This results in substantial debate within the U.S. environmental community concerning the qualifications of the individuals chargeable with this responsibility.

When determining the qualifications of the individuals who will identify and interpret regulations and voluntary standards, the implementation team should consider three factors. First, how complex is the organization? Second, how much external support can the organization expect? Third, how tolerant is the organization of legal risk? The first two questions are issues for the implementation team's consideration. The question of risk tolerance is an issue of policy. Here, the implementation team should seek direction from top management.

The best team for identifying the legal and voluntary requirements of the organization is an interdisciplinary one. The organization should use all its internal and external resources to help identify legal requirements and voluntary standards. However, once the team completes the list, the organization should consider a formal legal review. This review performs several important functions. First, it provides quality assurance. Second, it places in the hands of a qualified professional the final review, assuring that the organization meets its duty of care to review, identify, and understand and communicate all the regulations and voluntary standards applicable to it.

7 EMERGENCY PREPAREDNESS AND RESPONSE

The ISO 14001 requirements for emergency preparedness and response assure the organization that contingency planning and crisis management are integral parts of the business. The standard provides that the organization will establish and maintain procedures to identify and respond to accidents and emergencies. It also requires that the organization develop procedures to prevent and mitigate the environmental impacts associated with accidents and emergencies. These requirements help ensure that by setting up effective emergency preparedness and response procedures, the organization will reduce the number and severity of environmental impacts resulting from accidents.

Effective emergency planning and response assure potential interested parties that the business has planned for unexpected events and is acting as a responsible corporate citizen. By developing these procedures, the organization reduces the risk of accidents by considering the range of probable emergencies and their impacts, and preparing for those emergencies during normal operations, startups, shutdowns, and upset conditions.

THE STANDARD

Significant and often irreversible damage to the environment and health occurs because of accidents, spills and other unplanned releases. The costs of cleanup and damage control can be millions of dollars. The drafters of ISO 14001 and 14004 recognized these potentials when they integrated emergency preparedness and response into the standard.

ISO 14001

Definition

ISO 14001 does not define the term emergency preparedness and response.

14001

Section 4.4.7 provides that "The organization shall establish and maintain procedures to identify potential for and respond to accidents and emergency situation, and for prevention and mitigation of the environmental impacts that may be associated with them."

Further, "The organization shall review and revise, where necessary, it emergency preparedness and response procedures, in particular, after the occurrence of accidents or emergency situations." Finally, "The organization shall also periodically test such procedures where practicable."

ISO 14001 Annex

The annex does not discuss the issue of emergency preparedness and response although it indicates that the drafters may include text in a future revision.

ISO 14004

Section 4.3.3.4 suggests that "Emergency plans and procedures should be established to ensure that there will be an appropriate response to unexpected or accidental incidents."

"The organization should define and maintain procedures for dealing with environmental incidents and potential emergency situations. The operating procedures and controls should include, where appropriate, consideration of:

- Accidental emissions to the atmosphere;

- Accidental discharges to water and land;

- Specific environmental and ecosystem effects from accidental releases."

Emergency procedures should "take into account incidents arising, or likely to arise, as consequences of:

- Abnormal operating conditions;

- Accidents and potential emergency situations."

ISO 14004 also attempts to provide some practical help. "Emergency plans can include:

- Emergency organization and responsibilities;
- A list of key personnel;
- Details of emergency services (e.g., fire department, spill clean-up services);
- Internal and external communication plans;
- Actions taken in the event of of emergencies;
- Information on hazardous materials, including each material's potential impact on the environment, and measures to be taken in the event of accidental release;
- Training plans and testing for effectiveness."

ANALYSIS

ISO 14001 Section 4.4.7 directs the organization to consider the impacts of accidents, emergencies and unexpected incidents. ISO 14004 defines emergencies as incidents arising, or likely to arise, because of abnormal operating conditions and accidents. ISO 14004 identifies emergencies as accidental emissions to the atmosphere, accidental discharges to water and land and specific environmental and ecosystem effects from accidents.

Read as a whole, the standard identifies three mandatory elements. The organization must:

- Establish and maintain procedures to identify the potential for, and response to, accidents, operational upsets and emergencies;
- Review and revise procedures, where necessary, after an accident, upset or emergency has occurred; and
- Periodically test emergency response procedures.

Establish and Maintain Procedures

The standard requires that the organization establish and maintain procedures. These plans should include:

- a description of the emergency response team and its responsibilities; a list of key personnel; details of emergency services (e.g., fire departments, spill clean-up services); internal and external communication plans;

- actions the organization will take in case of different types of emergencies;

- information on hazardous materials, including each material's potential impact on the environment, and measures the organization will take in case of accidental release;

- training plans and testing for effectiveness.

In the United States, the Emergency Preparedness and Community Right to Know Act (EPCRA) and the Occupational Health and Safety Act (OSHA) and their state analogues require most organizations to have an emergency response plan if they handle hazardous materials. If the organization is subject to EPCRA or OSHA, it should determine whether its existing plans meet the requirements of ISO 14001.

Review and Revise Procedures

The organization must identify previous emergencies and operational upsets. The organization should then consider this data when reviewing its emergency procedures to reduce the possibility of a recurrence.

Periodically Test Procedures

The organization must periodically test its emergency procedures. Testing may include: desktop exercises; full-scale drills; evacuation exercises; emergency equipment testing; and and so forth.

THE LEGAL ASPECTS

This element of the standard raises three legal issues. A thorough analysis of the organization's emergency preparedness and response procedures may identify a prior noncompliance. Failure to develop, maintain, review and test the organization's emergency procedures may result in a misrepresentation to third parties who relied on the organization's ISO 14001 registration. A third party injured as a result of a breakdown in the emergency preparedness and response system may seek to discover the organization's emergency preparedness and response records to demonstrate that the organization was negligent.

Noncompliance

U.S. legislation already requires most organizations to develop an emergency preparedness and response program. The implementation team may discover that existing procedures are inadequate to meet regulatory requirements.

OSHA's Hazard Communication Standard in part serves as a basis for defining the scope of an organization's obligation under EPCRA. The duplication of process safety management requirements under the Clean Air Act Amendments for both OSHA and EPCRA regulations shows the inseparability of the relationship of workplace and environmental impact regulations. Various other federal statutes give the EPA authority over workplace activities. Examples include the worker protection standards under the Toxic Substances Control Act for asbestos and new chemicals. The Federal Insecticide, Fungicide, and Rodenticide Act provides similar authority for the protection of agricultural field workers.

Misrepresentation

Organizations registered to ISO 14001 say to third parties that the organization has an adequate emergency response program in place and that it tests and evaluates that program regularly. The organization is, therefore, making a statement upon which others will rely.

Should an emergency or operational upset result in injury to third parties, those parties may sue the organization for misrepresentation. The adequacy of the organization's emergency response plan will determine its liability.

Negligence

As previously discussed, negligence is the failure of the defendant to meet its duty of care in a way that is the actual and proximate cause of the plaintiff's harm. By documenting the adequacy of the organization's emergency preparedness plan through testing and post-incident evaluations, the organization may create a discoverable record. Plaintiffs may use that record to prove the organization breached its duty of care by failing to create, or maintain, an adequate emergency response plan.

Negligence per se

EPCRA and OSHA already obligate most organizations to establish and maintain an emergency response program. By creating a procedure to document the organization's emergency response program and performance, the implementation team may provide the evidence of the violation of a statute. If plaintiffs can prove that their injury resulted from the violation of a statute or regulation intended to protect the plaintiff from the type of harm suffered, they have established a prima facia case for negligence per se.

STRATEGIES AND RECOMMENDATIONS

The implementation team should consider both legal and procedural strategies to protect the organization from legal liability. These strategies include the legal strategies of privilege, amnesty and immunity; and the procedural strategies of adequate planning and documents retention policies.

Legal Strategies

Statutory Privilege

Some states extend their environmental audit privilege statutes to include audits of health and safety programs. The implementation team should carefully investigate such statutes to decide whether they can protect the information gathered in both the development and testing of the emergency preparedness and response program. The appropriate use of these privileges can protect the organization from both regulatory and civil liability.

Self-Evaluative Privilege

The drafters of ISO 14001 and 14004 require organizations to review and analyze prior accidents and upsets for lessons learned. If the plaintiff is a private party, the self-evaluation doctrine may protect these reviews from disclosure. The implementation team should seek legal advice concerning the applicability of the self-evaluative privilege in the organization's jurisdiction to establish guidelines optimizing the privilege's protections. The team should remember that this privilege does not protect information requested by regulatory agencies and prosecutors.

Amnesty and Immunity

If the implementation team discovers an existing emergency preparedness and response plan noncompliance, they should promptly correct the deficiency and consider seeking amnesty or immunity from the regulatory agencies. Again, this strategy will vary from one jurisdiction to the next. The team should seek the advice of legal counsel.

Procedural Strategies

Planning

In the final analysis, nothing is more effective in protecting the organization from legal liability than adequate emergency preparedness. In developing the organization's objectives and targets, the implementation team should verify that this element has received adequate consideration and financial support. The implementation team should make top management aware of the potential liabilities, and advantages, of committing the time and resources to make sure that the organization's emergency planning is adequate.

Document Retention

For ISO 14001 certification auditors, a log with testing data and scope and changes in procedures are sufficient. Most registrars do not consider the lack of background records a nonconformance. The implementation team should consider the development of a records retention policy that meets the needs of the standard and pertinent regulations without creating an undesirable document trail.

Practical aspects of implementing emergency preparedness requirements are further discussed in *ISO 14001 REQUIREMENTS, 61 Requirements Checklist and Compliance Guide* book by Jack Kanholm (annotated in the catalog at the back of this book).

8 SELF-EVALUATION OF COMPLIANCE

Every organization has an obligation to comply with some environmental regulations. The breadth of the regulation will vary from the large manufacturing facility to the small law firm. Nevertheless, these regulations exist and we are all subject to them. Compliance auditing provides organizations an opportunity to assure themselves that they are routinely checking, and meeting, their legal obligations.

Both U.S. EPA and Department of Justice policies recognize the importance of compliance auditing. Organizations that audit routinely and discover a noncompliance can reduce the legal impacts. Organizations who wait for regulators to find deficiencies face more serious consequences.

Although self-disclosure may be good for the soul, it also may have substantial legal risks. Federal policies intended to mitigate penalties for those who self-disclose do not impose the same restraints on state regulators or private citizens.

Audits that identify an environmental noncompliance may also lead to allegations of negligence per se. Organizations whose audits are incomplete or inaccurate may be liable for misrepresentation.

THE STANDARD

The standard requires the organization to establish and maintain a documented internal compliance auditing system capable of systematically evaluating the organization's policy commitment to compliance.

ISO 14001

Definitions

ISO 14001 does not define the term "self-evaluation of compliance."

14001

Section 4.5.1 includes the following sentence. "The organization shall establish and maintain a documented procedure for periodically evaluating compliance with relevant environmental legislation and regulations.

ISO 14001 Annex

The Annex does not discuss self-evaluation of compliance. However, it indicates that the drafters may include text in future revisions.

ISO 14004

Section 4.4.2 speaks to the issue of self-evaluation of compliance. "There should be a system in place for measuring and monitoring actual performance against the organization's objectives and targets in the areas of management systems and operational processes. This includes evaluation of compliance with relevant environmental legislation and regulations."

ANALYSIS

ISO 14001 Section 4.5.1 provides that "the organization shall establish and maintain a documented procedure for periodically evaluating compliance with relevant environmental legislation and regulations." Some have argued strict adherence to Section 4.5.1 does not expressly require that an organization audit for regulatory compliance. They argue the standard requires that the organization establish a method to learn the rules and regulations that are applicable to it and develop a management system to ensure compliance with those rules and regulations. This view is incorrect.

The standard requires a systematic assessment of compliance status concerning all applicable legal regulations and voluntary requirements, and nothing less. The discovery and correction of noncompliances is the purpose of this activity. Looking the other way will not mitigate the associated legal risks. The organization must find out whether it is in compliance or not. Otherwise, it cannot carry out its policy commitment to comply with environmental regulations or establish appropriate objectives to meet legal requirements.

To measure the effectiveness of a compliance management system, the organization must look at environmental compliance itself. By analogy, a certified public accountant cannot effectively audit an organization's financial management system by looking only at its written procedures. Ultimately, the accountant must look at the checkbook for evidence of procedural compliance.

Establishing and Maintaining a Procedure

To establish and maintain a documented procedure for periodically evaluating compliance the organization must first identify its legal and voluntary obligations. Chapter 4 discusses this procedure.

Next, the implementation team in conjunction with top management must determine the appropriate periodicity of the compliance audit. This varies based upon regulatory requirements and the actual, or perceived, environmental impacts and resources available.

The team must establish a procedure for the evaluation. These procedures must include a clear identification of what to monitor, how to conduct the measurements and what data to collect for the organization to assess its compliance status. The implementation team will need to consider how to organize the audit to take advantage of any privilege or other protection the organization wishes to employ.

Documenting the Procedure

What is adequate documentation? ISO 14001 Section 4.51 requires that the organization document its procedure for evaluating compliance. However, this leaves unanswered the level of documentation required. Must the organization document outputs to prove that the compliance management system is operating? Must the organization document the output verification to show that the system is operating properly? The drafters failed to fully resolve these issues.

Evaluating Compliance

ISO 14004 Section 4.4.2 requires the organization to evaluate its compliance with relevant environmental legislation and regulations. Thus, the drafters intended that the organization compare the factual data against regulatory standards to determine compliance. The standard requires the organization to evaluate these results to identify areas of success and identify activities requiring corrective action and improvement.

THE LEGAL ASPECTS

Self-evaluation of compliance raises legal issues for both the organization and the auditor. The audit may reveal a noncompliance or a failure to disclose a reportable noncompliance. The audit may also provide evidence of civil liability in the form of negligence per se or misrepresentation. Finally, the auditors may be exposed to liability for negligence

Noncompliance

It is troubling when information generated voluntarily, at significant cost and in good faith is used as a club against the organization who generated the information. It is especially troubling when it is very much in the public interest that the organization develop such information.

Compliance audit reports are particularly sensitive for several reasons. First, these reports have obvious investigative uses. A company that conducts a self-evaluation of compliance is essentially doing the equivalent of an agency inspection of the facility, thereby giving the organization the opportunity to recognize and correct any noncompliance. Such information, in the hands of a regulatory agency serves as a road map identifying possible noncompliances by the organization.

Government agencies can transform a self-evaluation, intended to help identify and respond to environmental impacts, into a document potentially capable of making the government's case against the company. In an era where knowingly violating environmental laws can result in criminal sanctions, including jail time for responsible corporate officers, the possibility that environmental agencies might use compliance audit documents to establish not only the existence of substantive violations, but knowledge of it, threatens many organizations.

The U.S. Department of Justice has used audit results to good effect in criminal prosecutions to prove the corporate management was aware of the existence of environmental violations and did not act to correct them when it could have done so. DOJ has consistently refused to limit access to audit results for criminal enforcement purposes.

Failure to Disclose

Many environmental laws have self-reporting requirements. The SEC also imposes disclosure requirements. EPA and DOJ and the amnesty provision of many state statutes mandate disclosure of noncompliances as a condition precedent to taking advantage of any penalty reductions.

The organization faces a dilemma. Failure to reveal a noncompliance is a separate crime and precludes potential penalty mitigation options. However, disclosure may substitute private civil liability for a regulatory noncompliance.

Malpractice

Failure to properly conduct an audit could bring legal consequences for the auditor. Although this is not an area in which case law is fully developed, courts will probably base the standard of conduct required for those persons doing an audit on reasonable care, good faith, and lack of fraud or collusion. "Reasonable care" requires that auditors use that degree of knowledge, skill, and judgment usually possessed by members of the profession. In determining the standard for the profession, a court would probably look to textbooks on auditing, government documents describing adequate programs and voluntary standards such as ISO 14010, 14011 and 14012; and existing standards of care applied to other types of auditors, such as CPAs.

Misrepresentation

An organization registered to the standard represents that it has a documented procedure for periodically evaluating compliance with relevant environmental legislation and regulation. ISO 14004 implies that the results of compliance evaluations will be used as the basis for corrective action. Organizations that fail to identify and correct noncompliance through the compliance evaluation process may be liable for misrepresentation to third parties.

Negligence per se

Compliance audits identify the environmental regulations to which an organization is subject and evaluates compliance with those regulations. As discussed previously, a plaintiff whose injury is traceable to the violation of a regulation intended to protect against that injury is well on the way to proving negligence per se.

LEGAL STRATEGIES

The implementation team should work closely and carefully with legal counsel to develop operational procedures and apply legal doctrines such as privilege immunity and amnesty to protect the information developed during self-evaluations of compliance. Because privilege, immunity and amnesty laws are in dynamic change throughout the United States, the role of counsel in providing current information is essential.

For obvious reasons, members of the regulated community do not wish to spend time, money, and effort doing environmental, health and safety self-evaluations only to provide state and federal agencies, and possible third-party litigants, the rope for their hanging. Questions of privilege associated with the performance of environmental audits are, therefore, of extreme concern to organizations.

As the implementation team develops procedures for conducting compliance audits, may consultants recommend that the team work with outside legal counsel. Organizations should consult outside counsel concerning two important issues. First, which privilege theories apply in the jurisdiction. Second, how to carry out the self-evaluation so that the organization may claim the privilege.

Use of outside counsel should reflect top management's appetite for legal risk. If the organization is highly risk averse or highly regulated, the cost of outside counsel will be acceptable. If the organization operates under a limited regulatory scheme, or if top management has a higher risk tolerance, they may choose to go it alone.

Once outside counsel has been selected, counsel should brief the implementation team on the privileges available to protect the self-evaluation. Again, these privileges will vary from one jurisdiction to the next. The dynamic growth of, and changes in, the self-evaluative and legislative audit privilege require periodic analysis by counsel to ensure a correct understanding of the law.

Statutory Privilege

Many states have now created a privilege for voluntary self-evaluation of compliance. Such state legislation generally extends the privilege to any administrative or civil proceeding for any report generated during a voluntary environmental audit unless the relevant agency otherwise requires the information. These statutes provide exceptions for violations discovered through such an audit but not promptly corrected by the organization. The implementation team must consult legal counsel to find out whether their state has an environmental audit privilege, how the privilege works and what it covers. This knowledge is critical to the development of a protectable audit program.

Self-Evaluative Privilege

The self-evaluative privilege stems from the public interest in encouraging companies to evaluate their past mistakes in order to prevent their repetition. The case law in this area is still developing. Legal counsel should review the law of the relevant jurisdiction with the implementation team. The implementation team should document that the purpose of the audit is to collect data for self-evaluative purposes.

Attorney-Client Privilege

Assuming that the only privilege available to the organization is the attorney-client privilege, the implementation team must work closely with outside counsel, structuring the audit to provide the greatest protection for the conclusions drawn. Procedurally, senior management should request a legal opinion of outside counsel concerning the organization's compliance with environmental regulations. Outside counsel then may engage consultants or organizational employees as its agents to collect the necessary information to render a legal opinion.

The attorney-client privilege is very narrow and only pertains to legal opinions. This has resulted in a myriad of court challenges to the assertion of the privilege. These challenges allege that the advice given was of a business rather than legal nature. The use of in-house counsel frequently blurs this distinction. Thus, judges are more likely to deny the privilege claim when in-house counsel provides the guidance.

Attorney Work Product

Courts protect documents containing the mental impressions of attorneys from disclosure so that attorneys can give properly researched and candid legal advice. Documents in which the lawyer intermingles his or her mental impressions are, however, the only ones eligible for this protection. The criteria to protect audit results under the work product doctrine are as follows:

- The organization must have prepared the audit in anticipation of litigation.
- The organization must not waive the attorney work product privilege by a breach of confidentiality.

■ An attorney must not have developed the materials in question to further an unlawful act.

Applying the work product doctrine to a compliance audit is problematic. The raw technical data created by the audit team is not the attorney's mental impressions. Courts only treat audits conducted in anticipation of imminent litigation and in preparation for the defense of that litigation as subject to the doctrine. Therefore, the routine self-evaluation of compliance required by ISO 14001 is not protected by this doctrine. However, organizations ineligible for some broader state privileges because a regulatory investigation has already commenced may wish to consider this option.

Amnesty

Besides privilege, many states — and to a limited extent the federal government — provide amnesty for information discovered during a self-evaluation of compliance. The conditions and scope of that amnesty vary significantly between jurisdictions.

Under the new and complex federal audit and disclosure policy, the EPA may grant amnesty for some civil penalties for a prior noncompliance if the organization meets certain conditions. These conditions are:

■ Systematic discovery through an environmental audit or other due diligence;

■ Voluntary discovery;

■ Prompt disclosure within 10 days;

■ Independent discovery and disclosure;

■ Correction and remediation within 60 days;

■ Written agreement to prevent recurrence;

■ No repeat violations or pattern of violations;

■ No serious actual harm results; and

■ The entity cooperates fully with the EPA.

This limited amnesty is discretionary with the EPA. The policy does not cover fines to recover economic benefit. The policy does not protect individual employees.

State disclosure policies vary broadly with about half the states granting some form of statutory amnesty. Other states, such as California, mimic the federal policy. Because these policies are changing rapidly, it is essential that the organization obtain counsel concerning the scope of any protection available and the procedure for invoking those protections.

The implementation team should consult closely with outside legal counsel to learn what amnesty options are available. After evaluating the options, the organization may opt to reveal otherwise privileged information, taking advantage of the jurisdiction's amnesty options. Finally, the implementation team should remember that they are always subject to the laws of two sovereigns. Amnesty granted by the state has no impact on the federal government and vice versa.

Immunity

If amnesty is the forgiveness of acts once openly declared, immunity is an assurance, before the disclosure, that the jurisdiction will take no legal action. Immunity is discretionary with the administrative agency. Some jurisdictions offer immunity for additional violations discovered during a self-audit as part of the settlement agreements and consent decrees. These consent decrees offer more mature industries an opportunity for a clean slate and the ability to move forward in a new self-regulatory environment.

Several states and federal demonstration programs have proposed an immunity provision. Most notably, U.S. EPA's Environmental Leadership Program proposes the provision of immunity for organizations that set up an audited environmental management system and maintain it for a minimum of three years. Some states are also discussing the option of prosecutorial immunity for organizations volunteering to participate in environmental management systems demonstration projects.

PROCEDURAL STRATEGIES

Three procedural strategies are applicable to minimize the legal risks emanating from the self-evaluation of compliance.

First, the implementation team, by conducting a through initial environmental assessment, can identify any organic system deficiencies that lead to noncompliances. Second, the team can design information fire walls. Third, the team can develop procedures for handling noncompliances when they are identified.

Initial Environmental Assessment Adequacy

Most of the risk of discovering and disclosing a noncompliance occurs during the initial environmental review discussed in Chapter 4. Because the initial environmental review is not a required element of ISO 14001, it is not auditable by third-party registrars and, therefore, is much easier to protect than routine self-evaluations of compliance. Later, as the organization becomes more confident with both its compliance posture and its environmental management system, the need to protect the information developed during the self-evaluation of compliance diminishes.

The initial environmental review provides the organization with a logical decision point. If the results indicate that the organization needs to concentrate on its compliance posture, top management can direct that the organization put the EMS implementation aside until the organization achieves an acceptable level of compliance.

Legislatures are constantly writing new laws. Regulatory agencies are continuously developing new regulations and policies. Thus, the more highly regulated the organization, the more serious consideration it should give to the legal strategies discussed above for every compliance audit.

Information Fire Walls

A second procedural strategy an organization can use to minimize the legal risk of compliance audits is to construct "information fire walls" between the information gatherers and the information evaluators. Information gatherers are those people in the organization who collect the specific data. "How hot was the outflow water?" "What were the particulate emissions from stack 47?" "When was hazardous waste first placed in drum 22?" Information evaluators are those individuals who draw conclusions from collected facts. "The temperature of the outflow water exceeds permit limitations". "The particulate emissions are within our permit's standards". "We have violated RCRA by storing hazardous waste beyond 90 days without a permit".

By bifurcating these tasks, protecting the organization is simpler. The fewer the number of people involved in drawing specific conclusions, the more likely a privilege will apply because it demonstrates that the organization intended the conclusions to be confidential.

The creation of an information fire wall between the data collection and data evaluation also allows top management to decide who will ultimately reveal any noncompliance discovered thereby reducing the probability of information leaks.

Advanced Planning

If the business discovers a regulatory violation during a compliance audit, the following are some considerations that the organization needs to address before disclosing the violation to the government.

First, the organization must correct the violation quickly or take reasonable steps to identify the source of the problem and create a corrective action plan. The organization must always show good faith.

Second, the organization must determine whether it has a legal duty to reveal the violation. The EPA's policy allows 10 days from discovery to disclosure. Ten days is not much time to analyze the facts and the law. Consequently, the implementation team should develop procedures allowing information evaluators to identify and communicate potential violations to top management or corporate counsel. Operations personnel must know who to contact, how to respond if a violation occurs, and what information the decision makers will need.

Third, information evaluators may require assistance from outside knowledgeable environmental professionals, including an environmental consultant and an environmental attorney. These professionals can help the organization decide what corrective actions to take and whether to make a disclosure to regulatory authorities. These professionals can also help the organization determine the range of consequences to decide what punishments, if any, are likely to be imposed based on similarly situated organizations that made voluntary disclosures.

Fourth, the organization should consider all the collateral consequences that may occur because of a disclosure. For example, third parties such as neighbors and environmental groups, who may have legitimate concerns and are entitled to information about the violation, may decide to bring their own citizen's suit against the organization. The EPA's policy does not bind these individuals. The organization should consult legal counsel to find out if local immunity statutes provide protection from such suits.

Fifth, the organization should consider how to eliminate the cause of the violation by changing the existing program. A dynamic EMS should have procedures by which top management analyzes and restructures the program when a violation occurs to prevent future violations.

Sixth, the issue of who should reveal noncompliance is an important and strategic one. Many disclosure issues hinge on legal interpretations applied to specific facts. The organization should create a multi-disciplinary team using its environmental experts to elicit the facts and legal counsel to apply the law. If the team believes a reportable noncompliance has occurred, it is desirable that the organization's legal counsel make the disclosure to the agency. Legal counsel is in the best position not only to delineate the issues for the agency but also to negotiate the best possible settlement of those issues.

A practical system for evaluating compliance is further discussed in *ISO 14001 REQUIREMENTS, 61 Requirements Checklist and Compliance Guide* book by Jack Kanholm (annotated in the catalog at the back of this book).

ENVIRONMENTAL MANAGEMENT SYSTEM AUDITS

An environmental management system audit verifies that the system conforms to the requirements of ISO 14001 and the organization's own policy objectives, targets and procedures; and that the system is properly implemented. The purpose of the audit is to provide top management with information concerning the effectiveness and adequacy of the organizational structure, responsibilities, practices, procedures and resources necessary for carrying out the environmental management system. An environmental management system audit is the ultimate, and probably only, evidence of the continuous maintenance of the environmental management system. Without the system audit, the organization has no proof that its EMS exists and is functioning.

The EMS audit also provides additional organizational benefits. They give the organization a clear snapshot of the organization's management system performance. They display an attempt to comply with the organization's internal commitments and societal obligations to the environment. They provide comfort to interested parties that the organization has a functioning management system in place that routinely considers and addresses its environmental aspects.

However, EMS audits can also create significant legal risks. As defined in ISO 14001 and 14004, the EMS audit is broad in scope. It covers all aspects of the organization's environmental management system. This documented review could be both the regulator's and the plaintiff's best friend in bringing a legal action against the organization. It could providing proof of top management's knowledge of environmental management system inadequacies.

Finally, ISO 14001 does not intend that EMS audits become compliance audits. However, part of the EMS audit is to ensure conformance to Section 4.5.1 (self-evaluation of compliance). Self-evaluation of compliance is a more familiar, and comfortable, role for traditional environmental specialists. Therefore, the implementation team must develop strategies to ensure that EMS audits do not degenerate into compliance audits.

TYPE OF AUDIT

Audits fall into three classes based on the parties conducting the audit. These are internal audits, second-party audits and third-party audits. An internal audit is one conducted by members of the organization being audited (the auditee). A second-party audit is one conducted by an affiliated organization. A third-party audit is an audit conducted by an independent organization. This chapter focuses on internal and second-party audits. Chapter 12 discusses third-party audits.

Internal Audits

The organization conducts internal audits for its own use. Their purpose is to allow the organization to evaluate the performance of its own EMS. Internal EMS audits are not self-evaluations of compliance. Self-evaluations of compliance assess the organization's compliance with regulatory standards. Internal EMS audits evaluate conformance with the organization's management system.

At least annually, an organization needs to internally audit its EMS to decide whether it conforms to both the organization's planned arrangements and ISO 14001. The audit team provides the results of the audit to top management for the purpose of review and possible changes.

Second-Party Audits

Second-party audits are those conducted by related or affiliated organizations such as customers, suppliers and insurers. Their purpose is to give the auditing organization a level of quality assurance that the organization is carrying out the EMS as designed.

102 ISO 14001 AND THE LAW

Second-party audits are probably the most dangerous. Second-party auditors generally lack the professional skills and training to conduct a thorough audit. They focus on specific aspects of the system and its performance that they perceive to be important. For example, an insurer's interest may be in superfund issues only. Thus its audit team may concentrate on emergency preparedness and response, skipping lightly over everything else. A customer's interest may be limited to regulatory compliance, making sure that the supplier will not be shut down or go out of business and that the supplier's liability will not become the customer's problem. Its audit team may focus on compliance rather than the management system.

Third-Party Audits

Third-party audits are an inevitable component of any ISO 14001 registration scheme. Third-party audits are what make ISO 14001 registration credible to outside stakeholders.

Auditors review the organization's entire EMS, including data reflecting self-evaluation of compliance to decide whether the organization conforms to the standard. Thus, while the mandate of third-party auditors is to review for conformance to the ISO 14001 standard, they cannot turn a blind eye to a regulatory noncompliance.

THE STANDARD

Definitions for environmental management system audits are found in ISO 14001 and 14004. Because they are such a critical element of the standard, ISO 14001, the Annex and ISO 14004 discuss EMS audits in detail.

ISO 14001

Definitions

Section 3.6 defines an environmental management system audit as "A systematic and documented verification process of objectively obtaining and evaluating evidence to determine whether an organization's environmental management system conforms to the environmental management system audit criteria set by the organization, and for communication of the result of this process to management."

14001

Section 4.5.4 requires that "The organizations shall establish and maintain (a) program(s) and procedure(s) for periodic environmental management system audits to be carried out, in order to:

■ Determine whether or not the environmental management system:

■ Conforms to planned arrangements for environmental management including the requirements of this International Standard; and

■ Has been properly implemented and maintained; and

■ Provides information on the results of audit to management."

"The organization's audit program, including any schedule, shall be based on the environmental importance of the activity concerned and the result of previous audits. In order to be comprehensive, the audit procedures shall cover the audit scope, frequency and methodologies, as well as the responsibilities and requirements for conducting audits and reporting results."

ISO 14001 Annex

Section A.5.4. provides that "The audit program and procedures should cover:

■ The activities and areas to be considered in audits;

■ The frequency of audits;

■ The responsibilities associated with managing and conducting audits;

■ The communication of audit results;

■ Auditor competence;

■ How audits will be conducted."

"Audits may be performed by personnel from within the organization and/or by external persons selected by the organization. In either case, the persons conducting the audit should be in a position to do so impartially and objectively."

ISO 14004

Definitions

Section 3.6 of ISO 14004 reiterates the definition found in section 3.6 of ISO 14001.

14004

Section 4.5.2 provides that:

- "Audits of the EMS should be conducted on a periodic basis to determine whether the system conforms to planned arrangements and has been properly implemented and maintained."

- "Audits of the EMS can be carried out by organization personnel, and/or by external parties selected by the organization. In any case, the person(s) conducting the audit should be in a position to do so objectively and impartially and should be properly trained."

- "The frequency of audits should be guided by the nature of the operation in terms of its environmental aspects and potential impacts. Also, the results of previous audits should be considered in determining frequency."

- "The EMS audit report should be submitted in accordance with the audit plan."

ANALYSIS

According to the drafters, audit program should consider:

- Activities and areas
- Audit frequency
- Associated responsibilities
- Communication of results
- Auditor competence
- How the organization will conduct audits

Activities and Areas to be Considered

Activities considered by the audit include functions and operations within the organization developed by the organization to carry out its environmental policy. Thus, if the policy contains a commitment to prevention of pollution, which it must, the EMS audit will identify all objectives and targets intended to meet this policy commitment and will then attempt to evaluate the organization's procedures for achieving its goals and targets and the effect of those goals and targets on achieving the policy.

The EMS audit is not intended to evaluate the organization's performance in achieving goals and targets. Rather, auditors use achievement of goals and targets as an indirect measure of the management system's effectiveness.

Areas refers to the various functions, departments or activities within the organization. The audit team reviews each area's procedures for achieving its related activities. Performance is audited only to the extent necessary to verify effectiveness of the system throughout the organization.

Audit Frequency

The standard does not provide any specific guidance concerning audit frequency. It directs that the organization schedule EMS audits based upon the importance of the activities audited and the result of previous audits. However, some periods are intuitive.

The primary function of the audit is to provide top management with information on the functionality of the EMS. (We discuss management review in the next chapter.) For organizations registering to ISO 14001, the national accreditation plan (NAP) requires the registrar to conduct a surveillance audit at least once a year. Most third-party auditors concur that the annual surveillance audit triggers an annual management review. Since management reviews should occur at least annually, it is common sense that the organization must also do EMS audits annually. However, the importance of the activity, the results of the last audit and the maturity of the EMS may dictate shorter periods.

Associated Responsibilities

Associated responsibilities refers to the procedural obligations of the audit team. From a legal perspective this may include: protection of privileged information; duties to reveal a non-compliance and nonconformances; and duties to protect the auditee's confidential intellectual property.

Communication of Results

The standard does not specify whether the audit team should communicate its results orally or in written form. However, the audit's identified uses (management review and as a baseline for future audits) makes it unlikely that in organizations of any size, conversations will be adequate. Further, verbal reports will be of almost no use to third-party auditors seeking to verify the organization's conformance to the standard.

Auditor Competence

The issue of auditor competence is tricky. Auditors, whether internal or external, must be able to do their jobs impartially and objectively. They should be independent of the activity being audited. For smaller organizations this may create a problem.

Auditors must be able to report the results of the audit. This implies that auditors have both adequate communication skills and language skills.

ISO 14012 provides guidance on qualification criteria applicable to both internal and external auditors. It specifies that EMS auditors have formal and on-the-job training. Formal training includes: environmental science and technology, organizational management, audit procedures and techniques and environmental law. On-the-job training includes participation in four separate environmental audits, totaling the equivalent of 20 workdays over a period of not more than three years.

ISO 14012 provides that "internal auditors need the same set of completeness as external auditors but need not meet in all respects the detailed criteria described in ISO 14012.

Conformance to the criteria will vary depending on such factors as: 1) the size, nature, complexity and environmental impacts of the organization; and 2) the rate of development of the relevant expertise and experience within the organization."

How Auditors Will Conduct Audits

The final requirement of this element is a consideration of how the audit team will conduct the audit. This includes: planning the audit; scheduling the audit; the opening meeting; the audit itself; the closing meeting; reporting mechanisms; followup and closeout.

THE LEGAL ASPECTS

EMS audits present three legal issues. First, improperly conducted, audits create the potential for misrepresentation. Second, the audit may identify a noncompliance. Third, the audit findings may show that the organization was negligent in the start-up and/or operation of its EMS.

Misrepresentation

Both the organization and the auditor should be aware that third parties may rely on the audit results if they are disclosed to the public. If the audit results are factually incorrect, both the auditor and the organization may be liable for injuries to third parties relying thereon. This is of particular concern for second-party audits.

Noncompliance

EMS audits are not compliance audits. However, auditors may, while conducting an EMS audit, stumble into a noncompliance. Should such an event occur, the auditee faces all of the issues discussed in the previous chapter on self-evaluation of compliance. Further, audits conducted by second-party auditors may create liability for both the auditors and the auditee based on a duty to reveal the noncompliance.

Negligence

The environmental management system audit raises the issue of negligence. Such audits may act as a shield proving that the organization actively attempted to meet its duties by ensuring that its EMS was functioning properly, identifying and reacting to the organization's environmental aspects and impacts. Alternatively, such audits may act as documented proof that the organization identified weaknesses in its EMS or significant environmental impacts and failed to act on that information.

LEGAL STRATEGIES

Even when the EMS audit does not implicate a noncompliance, the identification of an EMS weakness can provide proof of negligence or misrepresentation. As with self-evaluations of compliance, the organization should consider protecting its internal EMS audits through privilege doctrines.

Statutory Privilege

In those jurisdictions that recognize an environmental audit privilege, the organization should conduct EMS internal audits under the statutory rules of the jurisdiction to protect the confidentiality of their contents. Most states established their audit privileges with compliance audits in mind. However, in at least one state with a privilege statute (Texas) the state attorney general determined that the legislature intended to include EMS audits within the scope of the privilege. Many states used the Texas statute as a template when writing their privilege statutes. Thus, organizations in other jurisdictions may expect similar interpretations favoring the protection of EMS audits.

Legal counsel needs to fully brief the internal audit team concerning the existence of any statutory audit privilege and procedures to ensure that protection of the audit results. Whether the jurisdiction's audit privilege statute extends to second-party audits is a matter of legal interpretation. Legal counsel will need to render an opinion concerning the scope of the jurisdiction's statute. The auditor and the organization will need to agree on the effect of the statute. Legal counsel needs to be part of these discussions to assure that the auditing organization understands and agrees to follow the local jurisdiction's statutory privilege requirements.

Self-Evaluative Privilege

In those jurisdictions where an environmental audit privilege does not exist, the organization should consider protecting their EMS audits under the self-evaluative privilege. The privilege appears applicable to EMS self-audits. Self-audits are after-the-fact self-analysis of past environmental performance. The audit team can create its communication with the expectation of confidentiality. Without the privilege, a chilling effect on the internal EMS auditing would result.

It is unlikely that the self-evaluative privilege extends to second-party audits. The purpose of second-party audits is not critical self-evaluation. The organization cannot expect the communication to remain confidential because the usual purpose of such audits is to share the results with outside parties.

Finally, most courts will not uphold the self-evaluative privilege against the claims of a regulatory agency seeking evidence of a noncompliance. Thus, even where the privilege is applicable Courts may limit its protections to civil actions such as malpractice and misrepresentation.

Attorney-Client Privilege

The attorney-client privilege has little application to the EMS audit. The privilege only applies to communications intended to secure a legal opinion, service or assistance with a legal proceeding. EMS audits are a routine management function. Thus, convincing a court that the audit's purpose was to assist the attorney in rendering legal assistance associated with a legal proceeding will be difficult.

Finally, to protect EMS audits using the attorney-client privilege, top management needs to carefully structure and initiate them for obtaining legal advice. Legal counsel must manage the audit. The distribution of the results must be on a need-to-know basis only.

Amnesty and Immunity

EMS audits are not rigorous compliance audits. Compliance issues are so tangential to the EMS audit's main purpose that these audits may not qualify under EPA and DOJ penalty reduction policies. However, if the audit team stumbles into a noncompliance and the organization chooses to seek the limited protections of the EPA and DOJ policies, it should promptly correct and reveal any noncompliance discovered.

State amnesty statutes may extend to EMS audits. Where courts, or attorneys general, find such amnesty statutes applicable, the organization should take advantage of them. Unlike privilege, amnesty protects the organization from legal liability while allowing free access to the valuable information developed through the EMS audit. Thus, the organization can protect itself from third-party liability through prompt correction and share the information with internal and external stakeholders to improve its EMS and general environmental performance.

Legal counsel should carefully review any strategy involving amnesty before its application. Counsel can review the statutory law and policy of the jurisdiction and give the organization a prediction of the outcome resulting from the discovery of a noncompliance during the audit.

Second-Party Audits

Implementation teams should weigh carefully the legal implications of second-party audits with their senior management and corporate counsel. Probably, the organization should defer audits of this type until an effective EMS is in place. Alternatively, the organization may wish to end all second-party audits, relying instead on its ISO 14001 registration.

PROCEDURAL STRATEGIES

The organization may employ three procedural strategies to reduce the legal liabilities associated with the EMS audit. First, the implementation team can develop procedures to control the flow of audit information. Second, the implementation team can develop polices to assure that the organization appropriately trains auditors before they begin the audit. Finally, the implementation team can develop procedures for limiting the scope of EMS audits.

Communication

The implementation team should encourage proactive communications by emphasizing procedures to ensure that when the EMS audit identifies system weakness, it expresses those weaknesses to top management. These corrective action requests allows top management to act to correct system weakness and avoid allegations of negligence.

Training

Auditor training is an essential element of any audit program. Using improperly trained auditors can create technical, legal and organizational problems, especially when outside stakeholders rely on the audit results. Thus, there are inherently logical, and legal, reasons for ensuring that an organization uses adequately trained auditors.

Training is available from several sources. The best comes from organizations that also provide EMS training and ISO 14001 Lead Auditor training. Good training does more than teach auditors the auditable criteria of the standard. It also teaches them to think creatively, investigate objectively, and use evidence-based criteria to make judgments.

Some jurisdictions, such as California, have developed formal training criteria for voluntary registration of environmental auditors. The Registrar Accreditation Board operates a registration scheme for ISO 14001 lead auditors. However, a groundswell is developing within the environmental auditing profession for an independent certification program for all auditors. It is likely that such a certification will develop around the ISO 14012 standard.

Training for internal auditors should focus on the management system instead of regulatory compliance. For auditors who have spent their careers in environmental health and safety, this notion is a paradigm shift.

As with internal auditors, the proper training of second-party auditors is essential. The auditee should require that second-party auditors prove their qualifications to conduct the audit; to define audit criteria according to an agreed upon audit plan; to support audit findings with specific objective evidence; and to ensure confidentiality of the findings. One way to ensure the qualifications of second-party auditors is to require evidence that they have taken and passed a RAB approved ISO 14001 lead auditor course.

Audit Scope

Another strategy the implementation team may consider is to limit the internal EMS audit's scope to avoid compliance issues entirely using different audit teams to conduct compliance audits and EMS audits. The EMS audit team would rely on the compliance team's executive summary as evidence of the EMS's ability to identify and correct regulatory noncompliances.

However, when the EMS audit team confronts a compliance issue that cannot go unreported, the implementation team should provide communication tools separate from the EMS audit report. The implementation team should predetermine the distribution of the information in conformance with the legal strategies previously developed with legal counsel.

A practical system for internal auditing is further discussed in *ISO 14001 REQUIREMENTS, 61 Requirements Checklist and Compliance Guide* book by Jack Kanholm (annotated in the catalog at the back of this book).

10 MANAGEMENT REVIEW

Management review is the last section of the standard. It is the critical component for ensuring continued improvement of the system. Management reviews take a broad look at the whole EMS to determine whether it is meeting the organization's needs.

The legal benefit of management review is its function as a liability shield. It is proof that the organization, including its top management, attempted to analyze the organization's compliance posture and environmental impacts. When conducted properly, it is an assertion by the organization that while it may not be perfect, it has attempted to avoid foreseeable injury to human health and the environment.

The greatest pitfall for management review is its potential to provide documented proof that some later injury was foreseeable. This can occur when the organization identifies a noncompliance, nonconformances or EMS weakness and then fails to take adequate corrective action.

THE STANDARD

ISO 14001 and ISO 14004 provide an in-depth discussion of the function of the Management Review and the obligations of the participants.

ISO 14001

Definitions

ISO 14001 does not define management review.

14001

Section 4.6 provides that "The organization's top management shall, at intervals that it determine, review the environmental management system, to ensure it continuing suitability, adequacy and effectiveness. The management review process shall ensure that the necessary information is collected to allow management to carry out this evaluation. This review shall be documented."

ISO 14001 Annex

Section A.6 states: "In order to maintain continual improvement, suitability and effectiveness of the environmental management system, and its performance, the organization's management should review and evaluate the environmental management system at defined intervals."

"The scope of the review should be comprehensive, though not all elements of an environmental management system need to be reviewed at once and the review process may take place over a period of time."

"The review of the policy objectives and procedures should be carried out by the level of management that defined them."

"Reviews should include:

- Results from audits;
- The extent to which objectives and targets have been met;
- The continuing suitability of the environmental management system in relation to changing conditions and information;
- Concerns amongst relevant interested parties."

"Observations, conclusion and recommendations should be documented for necessary action."

ISO 14004

Section 4.5.2 describes the review of the environmental management system. "The organization's management system should, at appropriate intervals, conduct a review of the EMS to ensure its continuing suitability and effectiveness."

"The review of the EMS should be broad enough in scope to address the environmental dimensions of all activities, products or services of the organization including their impact on financial performance and possible competitive position."

"The review of the EMS should include:

■ A review of the environmental objectives, targets and environmental performance;

■ Findings of the EMS audits;

■ An evaluation of its effectiveness;

■ An evaluation of the suitability of the environmental policy and the need for changes in the light of:

■ Changing legislation,

■ Changing expectations and requirements of interested parties,

■ Changes in the products or activities of the organization,

■ Advances in science and technology,

■ Lessons learned from environmental incidents,

■ Market preferences,

■ Reporting and communication."

Some issues that ISO 14004 suggests be considered in the review of the EMS are:

■ How is the EMS periodically reviewed;

■ How are the appropriate employees involved in the review of the EMS and follow-up?

■ How are the views of interested parties taken into account in the EMS review?

ANALYSIS

ISO 14001 and 14004 answer five questions that define the management review. Who conducts the review? What should the review consider? When should the organization conduct the review? Why conduct a review? How will the organization conduct the review?

- Top managers must review the EMS for suitability, adequacy and effectiveness at appropriate intervals to ensure continual improvement.

- The management review should consider the possible need for changes to the organization's policy, objectives and EMS in light of EMS audit results, changing circumstances and its commitment to continual improvement.

- Top management determines suitable review intervals. However, the NAP requirement that registrars conduct surveillance audits at least once a year seems to make the management review an annual requirement. The organization may conduct additional reviews as necessary.

- Because an organization is a dynamic entity, changes in the EMS policy objectives, or other elements, may be necessary. Top management must update the EMS to reflect the status of the organization's business strategy to maintain continual improvement, suitability and effectiveness of the EMS and its performance.

- The management review process must ensure that the organization collects the necessary information to allow management to carry out this evaluation. Top management must document the review.

THE LEGAL ASPECTS

The management review raises three legal aspects. First, because both compliance and EMS audit results become part of the documented review record, the review can become evidence that top management had personal knowledge of a noncompliance or the foreseeable impacts on third parties. Second, the review itself may provide evidence of noncompliance. Finally, if improperly conducted, it raises the possibility of misrepresentation.

Negligence

The Annex suggests that the management review include documented consideration of audit results, achievement of objectives and targets, continuing suitability of the EMS and the concerns of relevant interested parties. This documented review may provide evidence that top management was negligent because it had knowledge of foreseeable injury to third parties and failed to act.

By examining and documenting conclusions concerning the adequacy, suitability, effectiveness and efficiency of an organization's EMS, top management creates a documented record of its participation in the EMS evaluation and their direct knowledge of any significant environmental impacts, noncompliances or system weaknesses. This record may provide the evidence that plaintiffs require for civil litigation by demonstrating that future injuries to third parties were foreseeable to top management. While some jurisdictions may privilege these documents, if available through discovery they remain legal dynamite because they provide evidence that the top management was affirmatively, positively and directly informed about existing problems, including noncompliance.

Noncompliance

As part of the review process, top management considers the results of compliance and EMS audits. Such reviews can provide documented evidence that a noncompliance occurred and that senior management was aware of the occurrence. Failure to report a noncompliance or act to ensure that the noncompliance does not recur could lead to criminal liability for top managers.

Misrepresentation

The management review is intended to be an internal activity. However this documented review has many uses beyond maintaining the continual improvement, suitability and effectiveness of the EMS.

The organization may also use it to report on EMS performance to external parties. Public companies can use information in the management review to support and supplement Securities and Exchange Commission filings. Insurers, banks and potential investors may use the management review to assess the environmental health of the organization and its potential environmental liabilities.

The standard mandates that top management conduct the review to ensure the continuing suitability, adequacy and effectiveness of the EMS, reliance on the review by third parties is expected. When the organization makes the management review available to the public, interested parties rely on statements of fact contained in the management review. The organization and its top management may be liable for misrepresentation if those facts are incorrect and this causes harm to a third party.

Even when the organization does not release the management review to third parties, an action for misrepresentation may be possible. The management review confirms the system's suitability and appropriateness in the same manner that the EMS audit confirms the system implementation and effectiveness. Thus the act of review by itself infers a certain statement of suitability on which others may rely.

LEGAL STRATEGIES

Each of the privilege theories previously discussed help protect management review documents. Some jurisdictions may grant amnesty to the findings of management reviews if the jurisdiction defines the EMS review as an environmental audit and if the organization promptly corrects identified noncompliances. The implementation team should carefully consider all local jurisdictional rules concerning privilege and amnesty with legal counsel. The implementation team can then design the management review procedure to reduce legal liabilities and maximize the review's effectiveness.

Privilege

The organization must strike a careful balance between making EMS reviews available for organizational growth and continual environmental improvement versus the protection of such reviews from outside interests. Each of the three privilege theories has a strategic role.

Legislative

Some jurisdictions with statutory environmental audit privileges may privilege the management review. Legal counsel should carefully review the scope of the privilege. Does it extend to private civil actions or is it limited to regulatory noncompliances only?

Self-Evaluative

When the management review touches on previous noncompliance, emergency conditions, upsets, or injuries, the self-evaluative privilege may be applicable. These reviews appear to meet the three tests of applicability. Such communications are an after-the-fact self-analysis. Top management can conduct the reviews with the expectation of confidentiality and maintain the reviews as confidential. The lack of a privilege has a chilling effect on top management's willingness to candidly review these issues.

However, the self-evaluative privilege is not applicable to regulatory or prosecutorial agencies. Thus, management should carefully consider the potential for regulatory noncompliance before relying on this strategy. Top management should consult legal counsel with hypothetical problems to understand the scope of the protection before its application.

Attorney-Client

The attorney client privilege has limited applicability in this setting. Legal counsel is not conducting the review. The review is not for giving legal advice.

However, to the extent that the review identifies a noncompliance, top management may wish to defer further discussions of the noncompliance and refer the issue to legal counsel. The attorney client privilege may then protect any additional legal opinions or advice rendered.

Amnesty

To the extent that statutory amnesty is applicable it is the best legal protection. Amnesty allows top management to evaluate and promptly correct any noncompliance without fear of retribution. This incentive encourages far-reaching, in-depth management reviews and correction.

The implementation team should, with the assistance of legal counsel, explore the applicability of any legislative amnesty within the jurisdiction and develop EMS review procedures accordingly. A word of caution: State amnesty legislation does not prevent legal actions brought by the federal government. Thus, the implementation team and legal counsel needs to develop guidelines for top management concerning the types of a noncompliance most likely to attract the U.S. EPA's attention and wrath.

PROCEDURAL STRATEGIES

Several procedural strategies are available to minimize the legal risks of the management review. First, the organization can engage in prompt corrective action. Second, the implementation team can develop document control and retention strategies. Finally, the implementation team can establish review frequencies intended to minimize legal exposure.

Mitigation

Beyond protecting the contents of the management review the organization must recognize its liability for failure to take action based on the conclusions of the review. Once top management identifies a regulatory noncompliance, it must act to remedy the situation. Once top management identifies a nonconformance with the registration standard, it must correct it. Once the organization identifies a significant environmental impact, it must consider the foreseeable harm and balance that harm against the cost of prevention.

If no solution to the potential harm exists, or the solution is prohibitively expensive, these procedures provide demonstrable proof that the organization considered the issue and made reasonable efforts to mitigate the foreseeable harm. Conversely, if the organization identifies a financially viable solution, the organization should plan for its accomplishment.

Documentation

While ISO 14001 obligates top management to document its review, it does not obligate managers to record for posterity every irrelevant comment or accusation. The implementation team should develop procedures intended to minimize the scope of the documented record. ISO 14001 requires that top management collect necessary information. The Annex identifies this necessary information as results of audits; accomplishment of stated objectives and targets; the continuing suitability of the EMS; and concerns of interested parties. Additionally, the Annex states that "observations, conclusions and recommendations should be documented for necessary action." Reading ISO 14001 and the Annex together, the minimum documentation required includes: 1) a statement of the documents received; and 2) a statement of observations, conclusions and actions. The final document should be reviewed by legal counsel and all drafts destroyed.

Senior management should consider the use of oral presentation as a method for reviewing necessary information. This method minimizes unnecessary documents and maximizes direct contact between top management and the organizational members charged with implementing the EMS.

The implementation team should develop a records retention policy. Most auditors consider adequate document retention of management review documents to be three audit cycles. However, the audit team should consult with the organization's registrar.

Older documents serve little purpose. The organization should destroy them in conformance with a policy approved by legal counsel.

Frequency of Review

During the early stages of EMS start-up, management reviews should be frequent, probably once a quarter. Short periodicity shows management's intention to identify and correct nonconformances and noncompliances.

Additionally, short review cycles make managing the maturation of the EMS easier. They help the organization stay on track and reinforce management's commitment to the system.

The implementation team can make shorter review periods more manageable by limiting the scope of the review. Top management may wish to concentrate on only one or two elements of the management system at each review and then conduct a summary review at the end of the year.

All requirements pertaining to management reviews are systematically discussed in *ISO 14001 REQUIREMENTS, 61 Requirements Checklist and Compliance Guide* book by Jack Kanholm. In *ISO 14001 Documentation* there is also a procedure for conducting management reviews . Both publications are annotated in the catalog at the back of this book.

11 LEGAL ISSUES FOR ORGANI-ZATIONAL PARTICIPANTS

The preceding chapters discuss solutions to the seven hot-button legal issues most likely to arise during the start-up of an ISO 14001 EMS. This chapter considers the ongoing legal issues that an Environmental Management System raises for various members of the organization.

This chapter divides organizational participants into six classes. These classes are Top Management, Corporate Counsel Management's Representative, The Implementation Team, Internal Auditors, and Everyone Else.

In smaller organizations these job functions overlap. However, this chapter considers each job function separately.

TOP MANAGEMENT

Top management consists of the individuals responsible for the development of policies. They control the resources necessary to carry out the environmental policy and are accountable to the outside stakeholders. When the registered unit is smaller than the entire organization, top management may delegate these functions to the most senior manager within that unit. However, delegated top managers must have the authority to both create and carry out policy. Thus, the standard raises two legal issues. Who is a top manager? What obligations does the standard impose on top management?

Who is a Top Manager?

Although undefined in the standard, ISO 14001 frequently refers to the obligations of top management. The Annex provides the following note concerning top management. "Top management may consist of an individual or group of individuals with executive responsibility." Unfortunately, the standard fails to define "executive responsibility" and, therefore, never answers the question, "What is top management?"

The standard implies a definition through the duties imposed. Top management sets policy, reviews results and most important, has the authority to direct the organization's work force and resources to carry out the policy and achieve the results.

Traditionally, these are the powers associated with the board of directors or the chief executive officer. However, ISO 14001 allows organizations to certify subordinate organizational units. Thus, the question arises: Who is top management in a subordinate unit?

For some organizations, auditors report a significant gap between the authority of those identified as top management and the authority required by the standard. This authority gap leads to significant concerns for registrars who must decide whether the EMS can function at the level proposed for registration.

Auditors and courts will scrutinize the job descriptions of the individuals. Are these individuals truly empowered to set policy? Are these individuals truly empowered to redirect the organization's resources to carry out those policies? Implementation teams and management's representative need to carefully, but diplomatically, review the authority of those individuals identified as top management by the EMS.

Top Management's Functions

ISO 14001 states that top management must define the organization's intent to reduce environmental impacts, while providing necessary support, and demonstrating organizational commitment to continual improvement of its EMS.

The first, and foremost, task of top management is to see the organization's environmental impacts in the larger context of the organization, its community, its nation and the world. Next, top management must take into account the organization's activities, products and services and then formulate the policy goals for the EMS to achieve.

Top management need not identify specific aspects and impacts. However, top management must review the resulting objectives and targets to ensure that adequate resources are available to achieve them.

Procedurally, top management meets these obligations by: appointing an environmental representative; developing an environmental policy; providing the resources to carry out the policy; and reviewing and revising the EMS to ensure the organization properly carries out the policy to accomplish its intended goals.

Appointment of Management's Representative

Section 4.4.1 obligates top management to appoint a representative responsible for conformance to the standard and performance of the system. This is a straightforward obligation. Simply stated, ISO 14001 obligates top managers to ensure that the organization charges identifiable individuals with the responsibility and authority to ensure that the organization's EMS conforms to the ISO 14001 standard, and for reporting on the performance of the system.

The higher the organizational rank held by the representative, the more support management provides to the EMS. To gain maximum results, management should assign the position to someone high enough in the organization to give the implementation team credibility and authority. Top management can optimize their representative's effectiveness by selecting an individual who is either a member of top management, or reports directly to top management.

Failure to appoint an environmental representative with sufficient authority to get the job done can undermine the entire ISO 14001 process. Top management should carefully consider, and document, it choice for this position to avoid future allegations of negligent entrustment.

Environmental Policy

The environmental policy is an organizational document outlining beliefs and practices that provide a focus for all organizational activity. Top management's involvement in this document is critical. It represents the environmental vision of the organization. Without inspired, clearly articulated leadership and vision, the EMS will flounder and, in time, fail.

ISO 14001 imposes five specific duties on top management in the development of the environmental policy. First, formulation of an environmental policy appropriate to the organization's environmental impacts of its activities, products and services. Second, ensuring that the environmental policy provides a framework for setting environmental objectives and targets. Third, ensuring that the environmental policy includes a commitment to continual improvement. Fourth, ensuring that the environmental policy includes a commitment to comply with environmental regulations and voluntary standards. Fifth, ensuring that the environmental policy is available to the public.

The policy is a publicly available statement of the organization's intended future actions and goals. ISO 14001 obligates top management to carefully scrutinize the policy to ensure that the organization's intentions are clear and the policy is not a misstatement of fact that could lead to a claim of misrepresentation by outside stakeholders.

Top management should carefully review the organization's environmental policy with the assistance of counsel. This review should not stifle the organization's commitment to continual environmental improvement. Rather, it ensures that the policy accurately reflects the organization's goals and aspirations.

Resources

Top managers approve the organization's environmental management system policy and make it available for public review. Implicit in any policy is a commitment by top managers to ensure that the policy will be carried out. Failure to provide adequate funding or staffing could be a misrepresentation. That is, the management said one thing but when it came time to fund the activity, management did another.

External Communication

The standard requires consideration of significant aspects and, potentially, their communication to external stakeholders. Such communications may lead to civil and regulatory liabilities for past acts. While the top managers have a duty to consider such external communications, the standard does not impose a duty to speak with third parties.

More troubling is the possibility that any documentation of top management's deliberations concerning communication to outside stakeholders may be discoverable. Top managers should consider strategies to protect these documents and the procedures required to invoke the necessary legal doctrines.

Management Review

Top managers have a duty to regularly review the organization's environmental management system and based on that review to reconsider policy and funding. Section 4.6 charges top management with reviewing the possible need for changes to the policy objectives and other environmental elements of the management system.

Through the management review, top managers are informed of — and responsible to consider — all problems illuminated by the EMS, including noncompliances. This prevents top management from claiming ignorance.

Failure to conduct reviews and to act on their results is a breach of the manager's duty of care. That is, should such reviews be inadequate or fail to occur regularly, any resulting injury may carry personal liability for the top managers and the organization.

CORPORATE COUNSEL

Neither ISO 14001 nor ISO 14004 mention corporate counsel's role in the development or maintenance of the EMS. However, ISO 14001 and 14004 discuss the organizations' obligations to:

- Identify, interpret and communicate applicable laws and voluntary standards;
- Commit to compliance; and
- Internally audit for compliance.

These obligations are sufficient to convince most organizations that corporate counsel has a unique role in the implementation and maintenance of the EMS.

For the purposes of this discussion, corporate counsel is not intended to be synonymous with in-house counsel. Rather, this discussion refers to the organization's environmental attorney.

Corporate counsel is generally identified as a part of, or employed by, top management. However, because corporate counsel's duties are so unique under ISO 14001, this discussion addresses the job function separately.

Corporate counsel has duties related to the planning and start-up portions of the standard. In addition, corporate counsel provides legal guidance to all other organizational participants concerning their obligations under the standard. Therefore, corporate counsel must be fully conversant with the standard.

As the organization plans and implements its EMS, corporate counsel has four important responsibilities. First, counsel is ultimately responsible for the identification of the organization's legal obligations. Second, corporate counsel must establish procedures for handling noncompliances. Third, corporate counsel must be fully conversant with available legal doctrines to protect sensitive EMS information. Fourth, corporate counsel must assess the organizations compliance posture as a result of information collected during the compliance audits

Legal Requirements

ISO 14001 requires that the organization identify and have access to applicable legislative, regulatory and other voluntary requirements. Corporate counsel is responsible for ensuring the proper conduct of this activity.

Disclosure of Noncompliances

Corporate counsel should establish a method for handling discoveries of a noncompliance with environmental laws or regulations by compliance or EMS auditors. This requires development of a decision-making tree that provides legal standards to decide what to reveal and who will reveal it.

Protection of Privileged and Confidential Information

Corporate counsel must establish adequate arrangements consistent with the applicable laws to safeguard the confidentially of information obtained during the development and operation of the organization's EMS. External auditors and registrars gain intimate knowledge of the organization's operations, strategies and technologies through the EMS. Much of this information may be privileged or confidential trade secrets. Corporate counsel is responsible for developing methods designed to protect privileged information and valuable intellectual assets without impeding the auditor's ability to perform their role.

Compliance Audits

Section 4.5.1 requires the organization to periodically evaluate compliance with applicable environmental legislation regulation and voluntary standards. This is the application of law to facts and can be done only by professionals with the appropriate training. While he or she may delegate portions of this duty, ultimately, corporate counsel has the responsibility to render a legal opinion concerning the organization's compliance.

MANAGEMENT'S REPRESENTATIVE

Management's representative is that organizational participant directly accountable to the top management for carrying out ISO 14001. Appointed by top management, he or she has authority and responsibility for:

■ "ensuring that environmental management system requirements are established, implemented and maintained in accordance [with the standard]"

- "reporting on the performance of the environmental management system to top management for review and as a basis for improvement for the environmental management system."

Who is Management's Representative?

ISO 14001 charges management's representative with the responsibility and authority to ensure that the organization implements and maintains its EMS in accordance with the standard. However, the standard requires that top management develop the policy, provide the resources, and routinely review and revise the EMS. Thus, management's representative must have formal power to command top management to perform its responsibilities. Only another member of top management can effectively perform this role.

In order to perform his or her function, management's representative must have technical competencies in management systems and environmental issues. It is possible for management's representative to rely on subordinates for expertise in the environmental arena. However, management's representative needs to be an expert in management systems. Thus, management's representative should be a member of top management with expertise in management systems and, if possible, environmental issues.

Management's Representative's Duties

Management's representative has three responsibilities. First, management's representative has primary responsibility for implementing the EMS. Second, management's representative must maintain the EMS. Finally, management's representative must report to top management on the performance of the EMS.

Implementation

As the organization implements its EMS, management's representative has four key responsibilities. 1) Management's representative must develop and implement procedures that ensure that the organization identifies significant aspects using a disciplined and objective methodology for evaluating the importance of those aspects. 2) Management's representative must develop and implement procedures that ensure that the organization considers significant environmental aspects in setting environmental objectives and targets. 3) Management's representative must develop and implement procedures that ensure that the organization considers the views of interested parties in setting environmental objectives and targets. 4) Finally, management's representative must develop and implement procedures that ensure that objectives and targets are consistent with environmental policy including a commitment to continual improvement, regulatory compliance and prevention of pollution.

Management's representative is responsible for ensuring that the initial environmental review provides adequate data to identify and evaluate the organization's environmental aspects. As discussed in Chapter 4, the initial environmental review raises significant disclosure issues for the organization. Management's representative is responsible for ensuring the development and use of strategies to protect this information.

Once the data is collected, it must be evaluated to identify significant impacts for which the organization may later establish objectives and targets. Again the organization faces the issue of disclosure of sensitive information. Management's representative consults with corporate counsel to develop and implement strategies to protect these discussions.

Management's representative needs to ensure that the views of interested parties are considered. An interested party is an individual or group concerned with or affected by the environmental performance of the organization. This duty leads to several unanswered issues. How is the management's representative to identify interested parties? Are lenders, insurers, stockholders and customers interested parties as well as neighbors and environmental groups? Whose views should be considered? What level of consideration should the organization give the views of interested parties? The drafters have not answered these questions. However, management's representative should carefully consider and document the procedures used by the organization in response to this element of the standard.

Finally, management's representative must ensure that objective and targets developed by the organization are consistent with the policy. This is a subjective judgment based on management's representative's training and experience. While no one expects management's representative to correctly evaluate all objectives and targets all of the time, it is important that he or she fully document the process.

Maintenance

Management's representative must ensure the establishment of a program for periodic environmental management system audits. As discussed previously, auditing without adequate protection has the potential to result in liability for the organization and its members. If the organization manages its EMS well, those liabilities should diminish significantly over time. However, the potential to discover regulatory noncompliance through an audit always exist. Management's representative need to discuss contingency plans with top management and corporate counsel to address the legal aspects of discovered nonconformities. That contingency plan should include pre-designed decision trees to respond to the following questions. Is there a duty to disclose? Is there a privilege that overrides the duty? If the regulations require a disclosure, who should make it? Are there options for obtaining amnesty or immunity? To whom should the disclosure be made?

Review

While ISO 14001 charges top management with the responsibility of conducting a management review, management's representative is responsible for ensuring that management has access to the necessary information.

Failure to perform this duty adequately may result in spurious conclusions by top management. However, the collection of the information necessary for effective management reviews may well provide a litigation road map for outside parties. Thus, management's representative must develop and implement a plan to protect this information.

THE IMPLEMENTATION TEAM

Neither ISO 14001 nor 14004 identifies an implementation team as a requirement of the standard. Rather, ISO 14001 provides that top management shall provide the necessary resources to implement and maintain the standard. The "implementation team" is shorthand for that bundle of human resources necessary to implement the standard. Larger organizations may assemble an actual group or team of employees to implement the standard. Smaller organizations may use a "virtual team" of outside resources and part-time staff to accomplish this goal.

Management's representative leads the team. However, he or she may need to look outside the organization for the multidisciplinary resources required. This book covers the legal aspects of ISO 14001 start-up. Therefore, it stresses the importance of legal support as part of the implementation team. However, an effective team requires many professional talents. These include expertise in environmental management, organizational management, information management, communications, health, safety, production, sales, marketing and finance.

Because the implementation team is the intellectual power behind the development of an effective EMS, failure to include all necessary disciplines can result in a system failure and potential legal liabilities. Management's representative should give careful attention to documenting decisions concerning the talents included on the team and the credentials of the participants to avoid future allegations that the team was inadequate to the job.

AUDITORS

Organizations are ultimately responsible for the conclusions resulting from internal audits. Whether the organization uses employees or contractors, both the law and ISO 14010, 14011 and 14012 requires that the individuals involved have both the professional and core skills necessary to conduct the audit properly.

Core Skills

Although this book treats compliance auditing and EMS auditing separately in previous chapters, certain core skills are common to both groups of auditors. Without those skills, conclusions of the auditor are suspect. Organizations using auditors who lack core skills may be subject to charges of negligence, misrepresentation or statutory violations. These core skills include interpersonal traits and objectivity.

Interpersonal Traits

Good interpersonal skills go a long way in conducting audits. Such skills include being able to interview people effectively, having a high degree of curiosity, adjusting smoothly to change, responding professionally to challenges to verbal and written statements, working well under pressure, and generally keeping cool. In addition, an auditor must be both a good communicator and listener. This takes sincerity, patience and a sense of humor.

Objectivity

Auditors must be objective collectors and interpreters of data. Implementation team members are always suspect as auditors because of the perception of a conflict of interest. It is true that the implementation team is only responsible for designing and establishing the system, not its operation. However, it may be difficult for others to make this distinction. When implementation team members conduct audits they will have the burden of proof concerning their objectivity.

Compliance Auditors

Internal compliance auditors are good detectives. Their job is to gather evidence that others can use to confirm or deny compliance with regulations and standards. They need three sets of formal skills: a working knowledge of the regulations; a familiarity with the audited facility; and computer literacy.

Compliance auditors should have a working knowledge of the applicable regulations. This is not to infer that auditors need to be trained attorneys. Rather, they need to have sufficient knowledge of the regulations to be able to follow audit checklists and protocols established by those trained to find and interpret the applicable law.

Auditors should have a familiarity with the type of facility being audited. This does not mean that to be an effective auditor of a chemical plant one must be a chemical engineer with twenty years of plant experience. However, one member of the audit team needs to have more than a passing familiarity with the how this facility operates and the common types of noncompliances that the team can expect to encounter.

Finally, auditors must be computer literate. The recent development of improved regulatory databases and auditing software makes computer literacy an essential skill.

EMS Auditors

Internal auditors must be knowledgeable of five basic disciplines. These are environmental sciences, the technology of the auditee, legislation, management system principles and practices, and environmental management. Because this combination of skills is unlikely to be found in one individual, teams whose members do encompass these skills should conduct audits.

Internal EMS auditors should receive formal training. There are private firms certified by internationally recognized organizations to provide auditor training courses. This training encompasses the requirements of ISO 14001, general EMS auditing techniques, and some training on environmental regulations where appropriate.

EVERYONE ELSE

Before the arrival of ISO 14001, management delegated environmental issues to a small minority of the organization. Frequently, management viewed environmental health and safety departments as surrogates for regulatory bureaucrats. They considered environmental health and safety as a cost center rather than a profit center. ISO 14001 expands both the benefits and responsibilities of environmental management to the entire organization.

This results in the distribution of responsibility for the EMS to every department, function and individual within the organization. The intent of ISO 14001 is to make environmental management part of every organizational participant's job. Just as ISO 9000 made quality job one for every employee, ISO 14001 makes improving environmental performance the obligation of every member of the organization.

However, the dispersion of responsibility brings a dispersion of potential of liability. Every member of the organization now must consider the environmental impacts and aspects of his or her job. How can the administrative support staff reduce the use of paper? How will maintenance staff ensure reduction of energy and raw materials? How will line management integrate pollution prevention into the production of products?

ISO 14001 makes each organizational member part of both the problem and the solution. As such, each member of the organization must be sensitive to his or her obligations for meeting environmental objectives and targets. The organization in turn must recognize that meeting environmental objectives and targets are part of an employee's job performance and reward accordingly.

12 LEGAL ISSUES FOR REGISTRARS AND AUDITORS

Environmental management systems address the needs of a broad range of interested parties. They also help meet the evolving needs of society for environmental protection. The EMS will typically encompass those environmental aspects that the organization can control and over which society expects it to have influence.

Registration of the EMS to recognized standards or criteria can provide confidence to customers, stakeholders and management. Third-party registrations may be tangible evidence of conformance to the EPA's audit policy.

The American National Standards Institute (ANSI) and the Registrar Accreditation Board (RAB) established an accreditation system in response to the need to accredit registration bodies in the U.S. to provide ISO 14001 registration services. The ANSI-RAB National Accreditation Program criterion (NAP), published September 13, 1996, specifies the requirements that third-party registrars operating an EMS registration program must meet to obtain recognition as a competent and reliable registrar. However, the NAP leaves many unanswered questions concerning the quality and consistency of both registrars and their audit teams. These unanswered questions may result in legal liabilities for both third-party auditors and the registrars that employ them.

AUDITORS

Audit teams are the eyes and ears of the registrar. Registrars charge these audit teams with auditing organizations seeking registration, confirming their compliance with the ISO 14001 standard.

Audit Team Composition

The heart of the audit team is the lead auditor. Procedurally, registrars report that they select a lead auditor for each registration or surveillance audit. The lead auditor:

- Selects the balance of the audit team;
- Plans the audit;
- Leads the audit team in the field;
- Reviews the objective evidence and conclusions of team members; and
- Has final authority over the audit report that he or she signs.

Because of the overall authority and responsibility of the lead auditor he or she has the greatest legal liability.

Auditor Liabilities

Legal liability for auditors is most significant in the following areas: professional malpractice; duty to reveal a regulatory noncompliance; disclosure of intellectual property; and, in the case of the lead auditor, liability for the actions of other team members.

Malpractice

Auditors are professionals. They undertake work calling for special skills and training. Where a person has knowledge or skills superior to that of the ordinary person, the law demands of that person a higher duty of care. Failure to meet that standard of care is professional negligence, more commonly known as malpractice. Auditors may be liable for injuries to auditee if the auditor fails to have, and use, the knowledge, skill and care ordinarily possessed and employed by members of the profession in good standing. Because the lead auditor is ultimately responsible for the actions and concussions of the audit team, this burden falls most heavily on that individual.

The NAP never identifies the specific professionals that should be part of the audit team. The NAP relies on ISO

14012 to identify the relevant criteria for audit team members. Registrars, in turn, delegate this responsibility to the lead auditor. However, the NAP does require that "When selecting the audit team to be appointed for a specific audit, the registrar shall ensure that the skills brought to each assignment are appropriate."

ISO 14012 states that "Auditors should have appropriate work experience which contributes to the development of skills and understanding in the relevant requirements of environmental laws and regulations. . . . In addition, auditors should have completed formal training. . . . Formal training should address relevant requirements of environmental laws and regulations and related documents." Thus, it appears that ISO 14012 and the NAP envisions formally trained professionals capable of evaluating each aspect of the ISO 14001 standard. Malpractice occurs when an auditor fails to meet his or her professional duty of care.

The auditor's potential liability does not stop with the client's organization. Lead auditors know, or should have known, that the auditee would use their audit findings to make a public statement concerning the conformance of the organizations EMS to the ISO 14001 standard.

The organization employing the auditor may also be vicariously liable for the auditor's malpractice if that malpractice occurred during the normal course and scope of employment or agency. Registrars have great potential for vicarious liability. Much like accounting firms, the Registrar may be vicariously liable for injuries to the public cause by the auditor's malpractice.

Regulatory Noncompliance

ISO 14001 Section 4.2.C requires that organizations' environmental policy include a commitment to compliance with the relevant legislation and regulations. Section 4.3.2 requires the organization to establish and maintain a procedure to identify and have access to legal and other requirements to which the organization subscribes. Section 4.5.1 requires the organization to establish and maintain a doc-

140 ISO 14001 AND THE LAW

umented procedure for evaluating compliance with relevant environmental regulations.

The NAP requires that the registration body focus on the existence of the organization's environmental management system and its start-up to ensure that it conforms to all ISO 14001 requirements, including its commitment to compliance with environmental laws and regulations. The NAP states specifically that "Data on compliance with relevant legislation and regulations gathered during the registration and surveillance is relevant and necessary to determine whether the organization conforms to the standard." Thus, auditors must verify that the organization has a system in place to identify legal and other requirements and to collect objective evidence that the organization's compliance evaluation system is operational.

Verification of the organization's compliance to Section 4.3.2 requires a level of legal expertise of the audit team. At least one member of the audit team should have the technical and legal background necessary to confirm conformance to this element of the standard.

The team can use technical experts to supplement their own skills if necessary. Alternatively, the audit team may wish to consider accepting an opinion letter from outside counsel. This document should outline the organization's regulatory compliance audit system; identify how and when audits occur; and the attorney's conclusions concerning the efficacy of the system. This approach allows the audit team to transfer both the costs and legal liabilities of this element of the audit to a legal professional.

Regulatory Disclosures

ANSI and RAB were obviously sensitive to the issues surrounding the discovery of violations in environmental laws and regulations by the audit team. "Because of the potential legal responsibilities associated with discovering a noncompliance with environmental laws or regulations during a registration or surveillance audit, the registration team shall establish with the organization to be registered a method for handling such discoveries." "Any method so established shall comply with relevant law." RAB calls upon the audit team to be sensitive to an observed noncompliance during an audit. However, RAB goes further. It requires the audit team to establish a method for handling such discoveries according to relevant law.

Pre-arrangements between the registrar's counsel and the organization's counsel may be sufficient to resolve these issues. However, auditors need to be fully briefed concerning their responsibilities and procedures to follow when they observe a noncompliance.

Frequently, registrars and registrants ask auditors to sign confidentiality agreements. These agreements often require auditors not to disclose audit findings, or other observations, to third parties. Many state and federal regulations obligate environmental professionals conducting third-party audits to reveal regulatory noncompliance and environmental contamination, especially if the noncompliance or contamination represents an imminent danger to human health or the environment. Thus auditors must assure that compliance with their contractual obligations does not violate state and federal law.

Trade Secret Disclosures

ANSI and RAB state that "The registration body shall have adequate arrangements consistent with applicable laws, to safeguard confidentiality and information obtained during its registration activities at all levels of its organization."

Further, "Except as required by the NAP, information about the organization, process or product shall not be disclosed to a third party without the written consent of the organization. . . . However, where the law requires information to be disclosed to a third party, the organization shall be informed of the information provided."

Again, the NAP requires the audit team to be sufficiently legally versed to make legal decisions in the field. What information must the audit team disclose to conform with the

NAP? What information, if any, in the registration body's possession does the law of the jurisdiction protect from disclosure?

Conflict of Interest and the Audit Team

ISO 14010 (Guidelines for Environmental Auditing — General Principles) requires that "in order to ensure the objectivity of the audit process and its findings and conclusions, members of the audit team should be independent of the activities they audit. They should be objective, and free from bias and conflict of interest throughout the process." The issue of professional independence is one of great concern. Obviously, if members of the audit team are not entirely independent, then interested parties may call the results of the audit into question.

The use of independent consultants who also provide EMS implementation services as members of the audit teams can result in a loss of objectivity or the appearance of it. Auditors may be working as consultants today and members of audit teams tomorrow. Worse yet, in some situations, registrars have sister companies acting as consultants, with no apparent separation between the organizations. Such activities undermine the credibility of the audit team and the registrar.

Liability Reduction Strategies

Generally, auditors can employ two types of strategies to reduce their personal legal risk. The first class of strategies are procedural. They include professional training, team selection and legal support. The second class of strategies is legal. They include indemnification and professional insurance. These legal strategies are most applicable to lead auditors.

Professional Training

First and foremost, each member of the team should know and be comfortable with the professional training and qualification of the other team members.

ISO 14012, as used by NAP as accreditation criteria, requires that:

- Auditors should have completed at least a secondary education, or equivalent.

- Auditors should have a minimum of five years appropriate work experience. Satisfactory completion of formal education may reduce the work experience requirement.

In practice, most registrars require significantly more formal training. Usually a bachelor's degree is the minimum criteria. In addition, ISO 14012 requires that auditors should have completed formal EMS auditor training and on-the-job training to develop competence in carrying out environmental audits.

Formal training should address environmental science and technology; technical and environmental aspects of facility operations; relevant requirements of environmental laws, regulations, and related documents; environmental management system standards against which audits may be performed; and audit procedures, processes and techniques.

On-the-job training should include 20 equivalent workdays of auditing and a minimum of four audits. This should include involvement in the entire audit process under the supervision and guidance of a lead auditor. This on-the-job training should occur within a period of not more than three consecutive years.

Finally, auditors should possess personal attributes and skills that include:

- Competence in clearly and fluently expressing concepts and ideas, orally and in writing;

- Interpersonal skills for the effective and efficient performance of the audit, such as diplomacy, tact and the ability to listen;

- The ability to maintain independence and objectivity sufficient to permit the accomplishment of auditor responsibilities;

144 ISO 14001 AND THE LAW

- Skills of personal organization necessary to the effective and efficient performance of the audit; and ability to reach sound judgment based on objective evidence.

Team Makeup

The audit team's composition should meet several tests. Does the team possess or have access to the necessary technical skills? Is the team able to work as a cohesive unit? Do team members have appropriate credentials? Are team members free of professional conflicts of interest?

When registrars and lead auditors assemble audit teams, they must have sufficient familiarity with the auditee to predict the technical skill required. However, if the audit team, as it conducts the audit, discovers that it requires additional expertise, the lead auditor must have authority to access those resources.

Team members must be able to work well together. Generally, the cohesiveness of the team is improved by member stability. Registrars should attempt to create a stable pool of auditors that can be mixed and matched to meet client needs. Technical specialists can then be added as required.

The lead auditor should be fully apprised of the credentials and professional experience of other team members before assembling the team. Through this process the lead auditor can assure that the potential for malpractice and conflicts of interest are minimized.

Legal Support

It is neither financially viable nor necessary that every audit team include an attorney. However, the team should have access to legal counsel throughout the process.

Legal counsel should establish the ground rules concerning disclosures with the auditee and communicate those rules to the team.

Counsel should be available to the team during the audit to respond to legal questions that may arise. Counsel should be available to assist the team in evaluating the auditees' conformance with the standard, especially Sections 4.3.2, Legal and other requirements, and 4.5.1, Monitoring and measurement.

Insurance

Finally, as with any other professional, the lead auditor needs to consider malpractice insurance. Doctors, lawyers and other professionals carry malpractice insurance. They do so because the provision of professional services creates a heightened duty of care and a greater potential for liability. As EMS auditing becomes recognized as a profession, lead auditors will require similar insurance products.

REGISTRARS

When an organization chooses to register its environmental management system, it hires a registrar to conduct a thorough audit. It is the registrar who engages the audit team who is responsible for conducting the audit.

The legal role of the registrar is analogous to that of an accounting firm. The accounting firm hires certified public accountants to conduct financial audits; the registrar hires auditors to conduct environmental management system audits. Although third-party EMS audits are new to the United States, the similarity of the structural relationship to financial audits provides guidance as to the legal duties, obligations and liabilities of registrars.

Misrepresentation and Malpractice

The role of registrars is to issue ISO 14001 certifications to registered companies. In issuing that certification, the registrar is saying to the world that this organization has met the requirements of the standard. Such statements can lead to liability for malpractice and misrepresentation.

Misrepresentation

The drafters intend the ISO 14001 registration to be a statement upon which others may rely. Thus, a registration issued to an organization by a registrar that negligently or intentionally misrepresents the organization's compliance with the standard is the first step along the path to liability.

If a third party, an investor, an insurance underwriter, a regulator, or a community member relies on the registrar's misrepresentation, and if that reliance results in injury, the registrar may be liable for the harm in the same way as auditing firms are liable for negligent or intentional misrepresentation of the financial condition of a company.

Registrars should confer with counsel to consider the scope of their liability, the ability to manage the risk through errors and omissions insurance or indemnification by the organization for the registrar's potential liability. Establishing specific quality control standards over auditors may help manage the liability resulting from incompetent audit teams.

These are business decisions balancing risk against profits. Should the team include legal counsel? Should the audit team insist on a comfort letter from the organization's legal counsel concerning identification of legal obligations? Is the registrar willing to absorb the risk of limiting the scope of expertise on the audit team in exchange for higher profits?

Malpractice

Not only do registrars have potential liability to third parties for negligent or intentional misrepresentation, they may also have liability to the organizations they audit for malpractice by auditors. Registrants rely on the professional judgment of the registrar's audit team. This creates a fiduciary duty of care for the registrar to ensure that the professional services delivered by the audit team meet the accepted professional standard of care. At this time, that standard of care is nebulous.

Registrars should consider carefully their procedures for identifying audit team members, their capacities and expertise. Additionally, registrars need to establish, either individually or as a group, a code of conduct and professional practice for auditors. Failure to do so may result in significant future liabilities.

Disclosure

The disclosure of information developed by the audit team during the audit may have significant legal impacts on the registrar. First, the registrar engages the audit team as either its agent or employees. As such, the registrar has vicarious liability for the acts of the audit team members.

Not only can this vicarious liability lead to civil actions for disclosure of proprietary information, in many states it may have criminal implications for the registrar under the state's environmental audit privilege legislation.

Registrars need to carefully consider with legal counsel the scope of their liability for disclosure and then develop strategies to reduce those liabilities. As with misrepresentation, the two primary strategies are insurance and indemnification. The registrar may wish to obtain liability insurance for injuries caused by its agents and employees. Alternatively, the registrar may seek indemnification by both audit team members and the registrant.

Appendix

Audit Immunity Legislation

As of April 1997, another 24 states have proposed audit immunity legislation: Arkansas, Alabama, Arizona, California, Delaware, Florida, Georgia, Hawaii, Iowa, Massachusetts, Maryland, Maine, Missouri, Montana, North Carolina, Nebraska, New Mexico, New York, Oklahoma, Pennsylvania, Rhode Island, Tennessee, Washington, and West Virginia. 28 Env't Rep.(BNA)331(June 13, 1997).

STATE	PRIVILEGE	IMMUNITY
Alaska	A.S. §09.25.475 (1997)	A.S. §09.25.475 (1997)
Arkansas	A.C.A. §8-1-301-312 (1995)	None
Colorado	C.R.S. §13-25-126.5(3) (1996)	C.R.S. §§13-25-114.5-126 (1996)
Idaho	I.C. §9-801-807 (1996)	I.C. §9-809 (1996)
Illinois	415 ILCS 5/22.2 (1996)	None
Indiana	I.C.A. §13-28-4-1-10 (1996)	None
Kansas	K.S.A. §60-3332-3337 (1996)	K.S.A. §60-3338 (1996)
Kentucky	K.R.S.A. §224.01-040 (1996)	K.R.S.A. §224.01-040 (1996)
Michigan	M.C.L. §3A.14810 (1996)	M.C.L. §§14801; 14809 (1996)
Minnesota	M.S. §114C.26 (1996)	M.S. §115B.8-13 (1996)
Mississippi	M.C.A. §49-2-71 (1996)	M.C.A. §§49-2-51; 49-2-2 (1996)
N.H.	N.H.R.S.A. §§ 147E:3-E:5 (1996)	N.H.R.S.A. §147-E:9 (1996)
N.J.	None	Title 13 Rev.N.J.Stat. (1995)
Ohio	O.R.C.A. 3745.70-71 (1997)	O.R.C.A. §§3745.70; 3745.72 (1997)
S.C.	S.C.C. §48-57-10-90 (1996)	S.C.C.A. §48-57-100 (1996)
S.D.	S.D.C.L. §1-40-35 (1997)	S.D.C.L. §1-40-33 (1997)
Texas	T.R.C.S.A.art.4447cc (1996)	1997 Tex.HB3459
Utah	U.C.A. §19-7-101-107 (1996)	U.C.A. §19-7-109 (1996)
Virginia	V.C.A. §10.1-1198 (1996)	V.C.A. §10.1-1194 (1995)
Wyoming	W.S.A. §35-11-1105 (1997)	W.S.A. §35-11-1106 (1997)

NOTICES

ENVIRONMENTAL PROTECTION AGENCY

[FRL-5400-1]

Incentives for Self-Policing: Discovery, Disclosure, Correction and Prevention of Violations

Friday, December 22, 1995

*66706 AGENCY: Environmental Protection Agency (EPA).

ACTION: Final Policy Statement.

SUMMARY: The Environmental Protection Agency (EPA) today issues its final policy to
enhance protection of human health and the environment by encouraging regulated entities
to voluntarily discover, and disclose and correct violations of environmental requirements.
Incentives include eliminating or substantially reducing the gravity component of civil
penalties and not recommending cases for criminal prosecution where specified conditions
are met, to those who voluntarily self-disclose and promptly correct violations. The policy
also restates EPA's long-standing practice of not requesting voluntary audit reports to trig-
ger enforcement investigations. This policy was developed in close consultation with the
U.S. Department of Justice, states, public interest groups and the regulated community,
and will be applied uniformly by the Agency's enforcement programs.

DATES: This policy is effective January 22, 1996.

FOR FURTHER INFORMATION CONTACT: Additional documentation relating to the
development of this policy is contained in the environmental auditing public docket. Documents from the docket may be obtained by calling (202) 260-7548, requesting an index to
docket #C-94-01, and faxing document requests to (202) 260-4400. Hours of operation are 8
a.m. to 5:30 p.m., Monday through Friday, except legal holidays. Additional contacts are
Robert Fentress or Brian Riedel, at (202) 564-4187.

SUPPLEMENTARY INFORMATION:

I. Explanation of Policy

A. Introduction

The Environmental Protection Agency today issues its final policy to enhance protection of
human health and the environment by encouraging regulated entities to discover voluntarily, disclose, correct and prevent violations of federal environmental law. Effective 30 days
from today, where violations are found through voluntary environmental audits or efforts
that reflect a regulated entity's due diligence, and are promptly disclosed and expeditiously
corrected, EPA will not seek gravity-based (i.e., non-economic benefit) penalties and will
generally not recommend criminal prosecution against the regulated entity. EPA will reduce
gravity-based penalties by 75% for violations that are voluntarily discovered, and are
promptly disclosed and corrected, even if not found through a formal audit or due diligence.
Finally, the policy restates EPA's long-held policy and practice to refrain from routine
requests for environmental audit reports.

The policy includes important safeguards to deter irresponsible behavior and protect the
public and environment. For example, in addition to prompt disclosure and expeditious correction, the policy requires companies to act to prevent recurrence of the violation and to
remedy any environmental harm which may have occurred. Repeated violations or those

which result in actual harm or may present imminent and substantial endangerment are not eligible for relief under this policy, and companies will not be allowed to gain an economic advantage over their competitors by delaying their investment in compliance. Corporations remain criminally liable for violations that result from conscious disregard of their obligations under the law, and individuals are liable for criminal misconduct.

The issuance of this policy concludes EPA's eighteen-month public evaluation of the optimum way to encourage voluntary self-policing while preserving fair and effective enforcement. The incentives, conditions and exceptions announced today reflect thoughtful suggestions from the Department of Justice, state attorneys general and local prosecutors, state environmental agencies, the regulated community, and public interest organizations. EPA believes that it has found a balanced and responsible approach, and will conduct a study within three years to determine the effectiveness of this policy.

B. Public Process

One of the Environmental Protection Agency's most important responsibilities is ensuring compliance with federal laws that protect public health and safeguard the environment. Effective deterrence requires inspecting, bringing penalty actions and securing compliance and remediation of harm. But EPA realizes that achieving compliance also requires the cooperation of thousands of businesses and other regulated entities subject to these requirements. Accordingly, in May of 1994, the Administrator asked the Office of Enforcement and Compliance Assurance (OECA) to determine whether additional incentives were needed to encourage voluntary disclosure and correction of violations uncovered during environmental audits.

EPA began its evaluation with a two-day public meeting in July of 1994, in Washington, D.C., followed by a two-day meeting in San Francisco on January 19, 1995 with stakeholders from industry, trade groups, state environmental commissioners and attorneys general, district attorneys, public interest organizations and professional environmental auditors. The Agency also established and maintained a public docket of testimony presented at these meetings and all comment and correspondence submitted to EPA by outside parties on this issue.

In addition to considering opinion and information from stakeholders, the Agency examined other federal and state policies related to self-policing, self-disclosure and correction. The Agency also considered relevant surveys on auditing practices in the private sector. EPA completed the first stage of this effort with the announcement of an interim policy on April 3 of this year, which defined conditions under which EPA would reduce civil penalties and not recommend criminal prosecution for companies that audited, disclosed, and corrected violations.

Interested parties were asked to submit comment on the interim policy by June 30 of this year (60 FR 16875), and EPA received over 300 responses from a wide variety of private and public organizations. (Comments on the interim audit policy are contained in the Auditing Policy Docket, hereinafter, "Docket".) Further, the American Bar Association SONREEL Subcommittee hosted five days of dialogue with representatives from the regulated industry, states and public interest organizations in June and September of this year, which identified options for strengthening the interim policy. The changes to the interim policy announced today reflect insight gained through comments submitted to EPA, the ABA dialogue, and the Agency's practical experience implementing the interim policy.

C. Purpose

This policy is designed to encourage greater compliance with laws and regulations that protect human health and the environment. It promotes a higher standard of self-policing by waiving gravity-based penalties for *66707 violations that are promptly disclosed and corrected, and which were discovered through voluntary audits or compliance management systems that demonstrate due diligence. To further promote compliance, the policy reduces gravity-based penalties by 75% for any violation voluntarily discovered and promptly disclosed and corrected, even if not found through an audit or compliance management system.

EPA's enforcement program provides a strong incentive for responsible behavior by imposing stiff sanctions for noncompliance. Enforcement has contributed to the dramatic expansion of environmental auditing measured in numerous recent surveys. For example, more than 90% of the corporate respondents to a 1995 Price-Waterhouse survey who conduct audits said that one of the reasons they did so was to find and correct violations before they were found by government inspectors. (A copy of the Price-Waterhouse survey is contained in the Docket as document VIII-A-76.)

At the same time, because government resources are limited, maximum compliance cannot be achieved without active efforts by the regulated community to police themselves. More than half of the respondents to the same 1995 Price- Waterhouse survey said that they would expand environmental auditing in exchange for reduced penalties for violations discovered and corrected. While many companies already audit or have compliance management programs, EPA believes that the incentives offered in this policy will improve the frequency and quality of these self-monitoring efforts.

D. Incentives for Self-Policing

Section C of EPA's policy identifies the major incentives that EPA will provide to encourage self-policing, self-disclosure, and prompt self- correction. These include not seeking gravity-based civil penalties or reducing them by 75%, declining to recommend criminal prosecution for regulated entities that self-police, and refraining from routine requests for audits. (As noted in Section C of the policy, EPA has refrained from making routine requests for audit reports since issuance of its 1986 policy on environmental auditing.)

1. Eliminating Gravity-Based Penalties

Under Section C(1) of the policy, EPA will not seek gravity-based penalties for violations found through auditing that are promptly disclosed and corrected. Gravity-based penalties will also be waived for violations found through any documented procedure for self-policing, where the company can show that it has a compliance management program that meets the criteria for due diligence in Section B of the policy.

Gravity-based penalties (defined in Section B of the policy) generally reflect the seriousness of the violator's behavior. EPA has elected to waive such penalties for violations discovered through due diligence or environmental audits, recognizing that these voluntary efforts play a critical role in protecting human health and the environment by identifying, correcting and ultimately preventing violations. All of the conditions set forth in Section D, which include prompt disclosure and expeditious correction, must be satisfied for gravity-based penalties to be waived.

As in the interim policy, EPA reserves the right to collect any economic benefit that may have been realized as a result of noncompliance, even where companies meet all other conditions of the policy. Economic benefit may be waived, however, where the Agency determines that it is insignificant.

After considering public comment, EPA has decided to retain the discretion to recover economic benefit for two reasons. First, it provides an incentive to comply on time. Taxpayers expect to pay interest or a penalty fee if their tax payments are late; the same principle should apply to corporations that have delayed their investment in compliance. Second, it is fair because it protects responsible companies from being undercut by their noncomplying competitors, thereby preserving a level playing field. The concept of recovering economic benefit was supported in public comments by many stakeholders, including industry representatives (see, e.g., Docket, II-F-39, II-F-28, and II-F-18).

2. 75% Reduction of Gravity

The policy appropriately limits the complete waiver of gravity-based civil penalties to companies that meet the higher standard of environmental auditing or systematic compliance management. However, to provide additional encouragement for the kind of self-policing that benefits the public, gravity- based penalties will be reduced by 75% for a violation that is voluntarily discovered, promptly disclosed and expeditiously corrected, even if it was not found through an environmental audit and the company cannot document due diligence. EPA expects that this will encourage companies to come forward and work with the Agency to resolve environmental problems and begin to develop an effective compliance management program.

Gravity-based penalties will be reduced 75% only where the company meets all conditions in Sections D(2) through D(9). EPA has eliminated language from the interim policy indicating that penalties may be reduced "up to" 75% where "most" conditions are met, because the Agency believes that all of the conditions in D(2) through D(9) are reasonable and essential to achieving compliance. This change also responds to requests for greater clarity and predictability.

3. No Recommendations for Criminal Prosecution

EPA has never recommended criminal prosecution of a regulated entity based on voluntary disclosure of violations discovered through audits and disclosed to the government before an investigation was already under way. Thus, EPA will not recommend criminal prosecution for a regulated entity that uncovers violations through environmental audits or due diligence, promptly discloses and expeditiously corrects those violations, and meets all other conditions of Section D of the policy.

This policy is limited to good actors, and therefore has important limitations. It will not apply, for example, where corporate officials are consciously involved in or willfully blind to violations, or conceal or condone noncompliance. Since the regulated entity must satisfy all of the conditions of Section D of the policy, violations that caused serious harm or which may pose imminent and substantial endangerment to human health or the environment are not covered by this policy. Finally, EPA reserves the right to recommend prosecution for the criminal conduct of any culpable individual.

Even where all of the conditions of this policy are not met, however, it is important to remember that EPA may decline to recommend prosecution of a company or individual for many other reasons under other Agency enforcement policies. For example, the Agency may decline to recommend prosecution where there is no significant harm or culpability and the individual or corporate defendant has cooperated fully.

Where a company has met the conditions for avoiding a recommendation for criminal prosecution under this policy, it will not face any civil liability for gravity-based penalties. That is because the same conditions for discovery, disclosure, and correction apply in both cases. This represents a clarification of the interim policy, not a substantive change.

*66708 4. No Routine Requests for Audits

EPA is reaffirming its policy, in effect since 1986, to refrain from routine requests for audits. Eighteen months of public testimony and debate have produced no evidence that the Agency has deviated, or should deviate, from this policy.

If the Agency has independent evidence of a violation, it may seek information needed to establish the extent and nature of the problem and the degree of culpability. In general, however, an audit which results in prompt correction clearly will reduce liability, not expand it. Furthermore, a review of the criminal docket did not reveal a single criminal prosecution for violations discovered as a result of an audit self-disclosed to the government.

E. Conditions

Section D describes the nine conditions that a regulated entity must meet in order for the Agency not to seek (or to reduce) gravity-based penalties under the policy. As explained in the Summary above, regulated entities that meet all nine conditions will not face gravity-based civil penalties, and will generally not have to fear criminal prosecution. Where the regulated entity meets all of the conditions except the first (D(1)), EPA will reduce gravity-based penalties by 75%.

1. Discovery of the Violation Through an Environmental Audit or Due Diligence

Under Section D(1), the violation must have been discovered through either (a) an environmental audit that is systematic, objective, and periodic as defined in the 1986 audit policy, or (b) a documented, systematic procedure or practice which reflects the regulated entity's due diligence in preventing, detecting, and correcting violations. The interim policy provided full credit for any violation found through "voluntary self-evaluation," even if the evaluation did not constitute an audit. In order to receive full credit under the final policy, any self-evaluation that is not an audit must be part of a "due diligence" program. Both "environmental audit" and "due diligence" are defined in Section B of the policy.

Where the violation is discovered through a "systematic procedure or practice" which is not an audit, the regulated entity will be asked to document how its program reflects the criteria for due diligence as defined in Section B of the policy. These criteria, which are adapted from existing codes of practice such as the 1991 Criminal Sentencing Guidelines, were fully discussed during the ABA dialogue. The criteria are flexible enough to accommodate different types and sizes of businesses. The Agency recognizes that a variety of compliance management programs may develop under the due diligence criteria, and will use its review under this policy to determine whether basic criteria have been met.

Compliance management programs which train and motivate production staff to prevent, detect and correct violations on a daily basis are a valuable complement to periodic auditing. The policy is responsive to recommendations received during public comment and from the ABA dialogue to give compliance management efforts which meet the criteria for due diligence the same penalty reduction offered for environmental audits. (See, e.g., II-F-39, II-E-18, and II-G-18 in the Docket.)

EPA may require as a condition of penalty mitigation that a description of the regulated entity's due diligence efforts be made publicly available. The Agency added this provision in response to suggestions from environmental groups, and believes that the availability of such information will allow the public to judge the adequacy of compliance management systems, lead to enhanced compliance, and foster greater public trust in the integrity of compliance management systems.

2. Voluntary Discovery and Prompt Disclosure

Under Section D(2) of the final policy, the violation must have been identified voluntarily, and not through a monitoring, sampling, or auditing procedure that is required by statute, regulation, permit, judicial or administrative order, or consent agreement. Section D(4) requires that disclosure of the violation be prompt and in writing. To avoid confusion and respond to state requests for greater clarity, disclosures under this policy should be made to EPA. The Agency will work closely with states in implementing the policy.

The requirement that discovery of the violation be voluntary is consistent with proposed federal and state bills which would reward those discoveries that the regulated entity can legitimately attribute to its own voluntary efforts.

The policy gives three specific examples of discovery that would not be voluntary, and therefore would not be eligible for penalty mitigation: emissions violations detected through a required continuous emissions monitor, violations of NPDES discharge limits found through prescribed monitoring, and violations discovered through a compliance audit required to be performed by the terms of a consent order or settlement agreement.

The final policy generally applies to any violation that is voluntarily discovered, regardless of whether the violation is required to be reported. This definition responds to comments pointing out that reporting requirements are extensive, and that excluding them from the policy's scope would severely limit the incentive for self-policing (see, e.g., II-C-48 in the Docket).

The Agency wishes to emphasize that the integrity of federal environmental law depends upon timely and accurate reporting. The public relies on timely and accurate reports from the regulated community, not only to measure compliance but to evaluate health or environmental risk and gauge progress in reducing pollutant loadings. EPA expects the policy to encourage the kind of vigorous self-policing that will serve these objectives, and not to provide an excuse for delayed reporting. Where violations of reporting requirements are voluntarily discovered, they must be promptly reported (as discussed below). Where a failure to report results in imminent and substantial endangerment or serious harm, that violation is not covered under this policy (see Condition D(8)). The policy also requires the regulated entity to prevent recurrence of the violation, to ensure that noncompliance with reporting requirements is not repeated. EPA will closely scrutinize the effect of the policy in furthering the public interest in timely and accurate reports from the regulated community.

Under Section D(4), disclosure of the violation should be made within 10 days of its discovery, and in writing to EPA. Where a statute or regulation requires reporting be made in less than 10 days, disclosure should be made within the time limit established by law. Where reporting within ten days is not practical because the violation is complex and compliance cannot be determined within that period, the Agency may accept later disclosures if the circumstances do not present a serious threat and the regulated entity meets its burden of showing that the additional time was needed to determine compliance status.

This condition recognizes that it is critical for EPA to get timely reporting of violations in order that it might have clear notice of the violations and the opportunity to respond if necessary, as well as an accurate picture of a given facility's compliance record. Prompt disclosure is also evidence of the regulated entity's good faith in wanting *66709 to achieve or return to compliance as soon as possible.

In the final policy, the Agency has added the words, "or may have occurred," to the sentence, "The regulated entity fully discloses that a specific violation has occurred, or may have occurred * * *." This change, which was made in response to comments received, clarifies that where an entity has some doubt about the existence of a violation, the recommended course is for it to disclose and allow the regulatory authorities to make a definitive determination.

In general, the Freedom of Information Act will govern the Agency's release of disclosures made pursuant to this policy. EPA will, independently of FOIA, make publicly available any compliance agreements reached under the policy (see Section H of the policy), as well as descriptions of due diligence programs submitted under Section D.1 of the Policy. Any material claimed to be Confidential Business Information will be treated in accordance with EPA regulations at 40 C.F.R. Part 2.

3. Discovery and Disclosure Independent of Government or Third Party Plaintiff

Under Section D(3), in order to be "voluntary", the violation must be identified and disclosed by the regulated entity prior to: the commencement of a federal state or local agency inspection, investigation, or information request; notice of a citizen suit; legal complaint by a third party; the reporting of the violation to EPA by a "whistleblower" employee; and imminent discovery of the violation by a regulatory agency.

This condition means that regulated entities must have taken the initiative to find violations and promptly report them, rather than reacting to knowledge of a pending enforcement action or third-party complaint. This concept was reflected in the interim policy and in federal and state penalty immunity laws and did not prove controversial in the public comment process.

4. Correction and Remediation

Section D(5) ensures that, in order to receive the penalty mitigation benefits available under the policy, the regulated entity not only voluntarily discovers and promptly discloses a violation, but expeditiously corrects it, remedies any harm caused by that violation (including responding to any spill and carrying out any removal or remedial action required by law), and expeditiously certifies in writing to appropriate state, local and EPA authorities that violations have been corrected. It also enables EPA to ensure that the regulated entity will be publicly accountable for its commitments through binding written agreements, orders or consent decrees where necessary.

The final policy requires the violation to be corrected within 60 days, or that the regulated entity provide written notice where violations may take longer to correct. EPA recognizes that some violations can and should be corrected immediately, while others (e.g., where capital expenditures are involved), may take longer than 60 days to correct. In all cases, the regulated entity will be expected to do its utmost to achieve or return to compliance as expeditiously as possible.

Where correction of the violation depends upon issuance of a permit which has been applied for but not issued by federal or state authorities, the Agency will, where appropriate, make reasonable efforts to secure timely review of the permit.

5. Prevent Recurrence

Under Section D(6), the regulated entity must agree to take steps to prevent a recurrence of the violation, including but not limited to improvements to its environmental auditing or due diligence efforts. The final policy makes clear that the preventive steps may include improvements to a regulated entity's environmental auditing or due diligence efforts to prevent recurrence of the violation.

In the interim policy, the Agency required that the entity implement appropriate measures to prevent a recurrence of the violation, a requirement that operates prospectively. However, a separate condition in the interim policy also required that the violation not indicate "a failure to take appropriate steps to avoid repeat or recurring violations" — a requirement that operates retrospectively. In the interest of both clarity and fairness, the Agency has decided for purposes of this condition to keep the focus prospective and thus to require only that steps be taken to prevent recurrence of the violation after it has been disclosed.

6. No Repeat Violations

In response to requests from commenters (see, e.g., II-F-39 and II-G-18 in the Docket), EPA has established "bright lines" to determine when previous violations will bar a regulated entity from obtaining relief under this policy. These will help protect the public and responsible companies by ensuring that penalties are not waived for repeat offenders. Under condition D(7), the same or closely-related violation must not have occurred previously within the past three years at the same facility, or be part of a pattern of violations on the regulated entity's part over the past five years. This provides companies with a continuing incentive to prevent violations, without being unfair to regulated entities responsible for managing hundreds of facilities. It would be unreasonable to provide unlimited amnesty for repeated violations of the same requirement.

The term "violation" includes any violation subject to a federal or state civil judicial or administrative order, consent agreement, conviction or plea agreement. Recognizing that minor violations are sometimes settled without a formal action in court, the term also covers any act or omission for which the regulated entity has received a penalty reduction in the past. Together, these conditions identify situations in which the regulated community has had clear notice of its noncompliance and an opportunity to correct.

7. Other Violations Excluded

Section D(8) makes clear that penalty reductions are not available under this policy for violations that resulted in serious actual harm or which may have presented an imminent and substantial endangerment to public health or the environment. Such events indicate a serious failure (or absence) of a self- policing program, which should be designed to prevent such risks, and it would seriously undermine deterrence to waive penalties for such violations. These exceptions are responsive to suggestions from public interest organizations, as well as other commenters. (See, e.g., II-F-39 and II-G-18 in the Docket.)

The final policy also excludes penalty reductions for violations of the specific terms of any order, consent agreement, or plea agreement. (See, II-E- 60 in the Docket.) Once a consent agreement has been negotiated, there is little incentive to comply if there are no sanctions for violating its specific requirements. The exclusion in this section applies to violations of the terms of any response, removal or remedial action covered by a written agreement.

8. Cooperation

Under Section D(9), the regulated entity must cooperate as required by EPA and provide information necessary to determine the applicability of the policy. This condition is largely unchanged from the interim policy. In the final policy, however, the Agency has added that "cooperation" includes *66710 assistance in determining the facts of any related violations suggested by the disclosure, as well as of the disclosed violation itself. This was added to allow the agency to obtain information about any violations indicated by the disclosure, even where the violation is not initially identified by the regulated entity.

F. Opposition to Privilege

The Agency remains firmly opposed to the establishment of a statutory evidentiary privilege for environmental audits for the following reasons:

1. Privilege, by definition, invites secrecy, instead of the openness needed to build public trust in industry's ability to self-police. American law reflects the high value that the public places on fair access to the facts. The Supreme Court, for example, has said of privileges

that, "[w]hatever their origins, these exceptions to the demand for every man's evidence are not lightly created nor expansively construed, for they are in derogation of the search for truth." United States v. Nixon, 418 U.S. 683 (1974). Federal courts have unanimously refused to recognize a privilege for environmental audits in the context of government investigations. See, e.g., United States v. Dexter, 132 F.R.D. 8, 9-10 (D.Conn. 1990) (application of a privilege "would effectively impede [EPA's] ability to enforce the Clean Water Act, and would be contrary to stated public policy.")

2. Eighteen months have failed to produce any evidence that a privilege is needed. Public testimony on the interim policy confirmed that EPA rarely uses audit reports as evidence. Furthermore, surveys demonstrate that environmental auditing has expanded rapidly over the past decade without the stimulus of a privilege. Most recently, the 1995 Price Waterhouse survey found that those few large or mid-sized companies that do not audit generally do not perceive any need to; concern about confidentiality ranked as one of the least important factors in their decisions.

3. A privilege would invite defendants to claim as "audit" material almost any evidence the government needed to establish a violation or determine who was responsible. For example, most audit privilege bills under consideration in federal and state legislatures would arguably protect factual information — such as health studies or contaminated sediment data — and not just the conclusions of the auditors. While the government might have access to required monitoring data under the law, as some industry commenters have suggested, a privilege of that nature would cloak underlying facts needed to determine whether such data were accurate.

4. An audit privilege would breed litigation, as both parties struggled to determine what material fell within its scope. The problem is compounded by the lack of any clear national standard for audits. The "in camera" (i.e., non-public) proceedings used to resolve these disputes under some statutory schemes would result in a series of time-consuming, expensive mini-trials.

5. The Agency's policy eliminates the need for any privilege as against the government, by reducing civil penalties and criminal liability for those companies that audit, disclose and correct violations. The 1995 Price Waterhouse survey indicated that companies would expand their auditing programs in exchange for the kind of incentives that EPA provides in its policy.

6. Finally, audit privileges are strongly opposed by the law enforcement community, including the National District Attorneys Association, as well as by public interest groups. (See, e.g., Docket, II-C-21, II-C-28, II-C-52, IV-G- 10, II-C-25, II-C-33, II-C-52, II-C-48, and II-G-13 through II-G-24.)

G. Effect on States

The final policy reflects EPA's desire to develop fair and effective incentives for self-policing that will have practical value to states that share responsibility for enforcing federal environmental laws. To that end, the Agency has consulted closely with state officials in developing this policy, through a series of special meetings and conference calls in addition to the extensive opportunity for public comment. As a result, EPA believes its final policy is grounded in common-sense principles that should prove useful in the development of state programs and policies.

As always, states are encouraged to experiment with different approaches that do not jeopardize the fundamental national interest in assuring that violations of federal law do not threaten the public health or the environment, or make it profitable not to comply. The Agency remains opposed to state legislation that does not include these basic protections, and reserves its right to bring independent action against regulated entities for violations of federal law that threaten human health or the environment, reflect criminal conduct or repeated noncompliance, or allow one company to make a substantial profit at the expense of its law-abiding competitors. Where a state has obtained appropriate sanctions needed to deter such misconduct, there is no need for EPA action.

H. Scope of Policy

EPA has developed this document as a policy to guide settlement actions. EPA employees will be expected to follow this policy, and the Agency will take steps to assure national consistency in application. For example, the Agency will make public any compliance agreements reached under this policy, in order to provide the regulated community with fair notice of decisions and greater accountability to affected communities. Many in the regulated community recommended that the Agency convert the policy into a regulation because they felt it might ensure greater consistency and predictability. While EPA is taking steps to ensure consistency and predictability and believes that it will be successful, the Agency will consider this issue and will provide notice if it determines that a rulemaking is appropriate.

II. Statement of Policy: Incentives for Self-Policing

Discovery, Disclosure, Correction and Prevention

A. Purpose

This policy is designed to enhance protection of human health and the environment by encouraging regulated entities to voluntarily discover, disclose, correct and prevent violations of federal environmental requirements.

B. Definitions

For purposes of this policy, the following definitions apply:

"Environmental Audit" has the definition given to it in EPA's 1986 audit policy on environmental auditing, i.e., "a systematic, documented, periodic and objective review by regulated entities of facility operations and practices related to meeting environmental requirements."

"Due Diligence" encompasses the regulated entity's systematic efforts, appropriate to the size and nature of its business, to prevent, detect and correct violations through all of the following:

(a) Compliance policies, standards and procedures that identify how employees and agents are to meet the requirements of laws, regulations, permits and other sources of authority for environmental requirements;

(b) Assignment of overall responsibility for overseeing compliance with policies, standards, and procedures, and assignment of specific responsibility for assuring compliance at each facility or operation;

*66711 (c) Mechanisms for systematically assuring that compliance policies, standards and procedures are being carried out, including monitoring and auditing systems reasonably designed to detect and correct violations, periodic evaluation of the overall performance of the compliance management system, and a means for employees or agents to report violations of environmental requirements without fear of retaliation;

(d) Efforts to communicate effectively the regulated entity's standards and procedures to all employees and other agents;

(e) Appropriate incentives to managers and employees to perform in accordance with the compliance policies, standards and procedures, including consistent enforcement through appropriate disciplinary mechanisms; and

(f) Procedures for the prompt and appropriate correction of any violations, and any necessary modifications to the regulated entity's program to prevent future violations.

"Environmental audit report" means the analysis, conclusions, and recommendations resulting from an environmental audit, but does not include data obtained in, or testimonial evidence concerning, the environmental audit.

"Gravity-based penalties" are that portion of a penalty over and above the economic benefit., i.e., the punitive portion of the penalty, rather than that portion representing a defendant's economic gain from non-compliance. (For further discussion of this concept, see "A Framework for Statute-Specific Approaches to Penalty Assessments", #GM-22, 1980, U.S. EPA General Enforcement Policy Compendium).

"Regulated entity" means any entity, including a federal, state or municipal agency or facility, regulated under federal environmental laws.

C. Incentives for Self-Policing

1. No Gravity-Based Penalties

Where the regulated entity establishes that it satisfies all of the conditions of Section D of the policy, EPA will not seek gravity-based penalties for violations of federal environmental requirements.

2. Reduction of Gravity-Based Penalties by 75%

EPA will reduce gravity-based penalties for violations of federal environmental requirements by 75% so long as the regulated entity satisfies all of the conditions of Section D(2) through D(9) below.

3. No Criminal Recommendations

(a) EPA will not recommend to the Department of Justice or other prosecuting authority that criminal charges be brought against a regulated entity where EPA determines that all of the conditions in Section D are satisfied, so long as the violation does not demonstrate or involve:

(i) a prevalent management philosophy or practice that concealed or condoned environmental violations; or

(ii) high-level corporate officials' or managers' conscious involvement in, or willful blindness to, the violations.

(b) Whether or not EPA refers the regulated entity for criminal prosecution under this section, the Agency reserves the right to recommend prosecution for the criminal acts of individual managers or employees under existing policies guiding the exercise of enforcement discretion.

4. No Routine Request for Audits

EPA will not request or use an environmental audit report to initiate a civil or criminal investigation of the entity. For example, EPA will not request an environmental audit report in routine inspections. If the Agency has independent reason to believe that a violation has occurred, however, EPA may seek any information relevant to identifying violations or determining liability or extent of harm.

D. Conditions

1. Systematic Discovery

The violation was discovered through:

(a) an environmental audit; or

(b) an objective, documented, systematic procedure or practice reflecting the regulated entity's due diligence in preventing, detecting, and correcting violations. The regulated entity must provide accurate and complete documentation to the Agency as to how it exercises due diligence to prevent, detect and correct violations according to the criteria for due diligence outlined in Section B. EPA may require as a condition of penalty mitigation that a description of the regulated entity's due diligence efforts be made publicly available.

2. Voluntary Discovery

The violation was identified voluntarily, and not through a legally mandated monitoring or sampling requirement prescribed by statute, regulation, permit, judicial or administrative order, or consent agreement. For example, the policy does not apply to:

(a) emissions violations detected through a continuous emissions monitor (or alternative monitor established in a permit) where any such monitoring is required;

(b) violations of National Pollutant Discharge Elimination System (NPDES) discharge limits detected through required sampling or monitoring;

(c) violations discovered through a compliance audit required to be performed by the terms of a consent order or settlement agreement.

3. Prompt Disclosure

The regulated entity fully discloses a specific violation within 10 days (or such shorter period provided by law) after it has discovered that the violation has occurred, or may have occurred, in writing to EPA;

4. Discovery and Disclosure Independent of Government or Third Party Plaintiff

The violation must also be identified and disclosed by the regulated entity prior to:

(a) the commencement of a federal, state or local agency inspection or investigation, or the issuance by such agency of an information request to the regulated entity;

(b) notice of a citizen suit;

(c) the filing of a complaint by a third party;

(d) the reporting of the violation to EPA (or other government agency) by a "whistleblower" employee, rather than by one authorized to speak on behalf of the regulated entity; or

(e) imminent discovery of the violation by a regulatory agency;

5. Correction and Remediation

The regulated entity corrects the violation within 60 days, certifies in writing that violations have been corrected, and takes appropriate measures as determined by EPA to remedy any environmental or human harm due to the violation. If more than 60 days will be needed to correct the violation(s), the regulated entity must so notify EPA in writing before the 60-day period has passed. Where appropriate, EPA may require that to satisfy conditions 5 and 6, a regulated entity enter into a publicly available written agreement, administrative consent order or judicial consent decree, particularly where compliance or remedial measures are complex or a lengthy schedule for attaining and maintaining compliance or remediating harm is required;

6. Prevent Recurrence

The regulated entity agrees in writing to take steps to prevent a recurrence of the violation, which may include improvements to its environmental auditing or due diligence efforts;

*66712 7. No Repeat Violations

The specific violation (or closely related violation) has not occurred previously within the past three years at the same facility, or is not part of a pattern of federal, state or local violations by the facility's parent organization (if any), which have occurred within the past five years. For the purposes of this section, a violation is:

(a) any violation of federal, state or local environmental law identified in a judicial or administrative order, consent agreement or order, complaint, or notice of violation, conviction or plea agreement; or

(b) any act or omission for which the regulated entity has previously received penalty mitigation from EPA or a state or local agency.

8. Other Violations Excluded

The violation is not one which (i) resulted in serious actual harm, or may have presented an imminent and substantial endangerment to, human health or the environment, or (ii) violates the specific terms of any judicial or administrative order, or consent agreement.

9. Cooperation

The regulated entity cooperates as requested by EPA and provides such information as is necessary and requested by EPA to determine applicability of this policy. Cooperation includes, at a minimum, providing all requested documents and access to employees and assistance in investigating the violation, any noncompliance problems related to the disclosure, and any environmental consequences related to the violations.

E. Economic Benefit

EPA will retain its full discretion to recover any economic benefit gained as a result of noncompliance to preserve a "level playing field" in which violators do not gain a competitive advantage over regulated entities that do comply. EPA may forgive the entire penalty for violations which meet conditions 1 through 9 in section D and, in the Agency's opinion, do not merit any penalty due to the insignificant amount of any economic benefit.

F. Effect on State Law, Regulation or Policy

EPA will work closely with states to encourage their adoption of policies that reflect the incentives and conditions outlined in this policy. EPA remains firmly opposed to statutory environmental audit privileges that shield evidence of environmental violations and undermine the public's right to know, as well as to blanket immunities for violations that reflect criminal conduct, present serious threats or actual harm to health and the environment, allow noncomplying companies to gain an economic advantage over their competitors, or reflect a repeated failure to comply with federal law. EPA will work with states to address any provisions of state audit privilege or immunity laws that are inconsistent with this policy, and which may prevent a timely and appropriate response to significant environmental violations. The Agency reserves its right to take necessary actions to protect public health or the environment by enforcing against any violations of federal law.

G. Applicability

(1) This policy applies to the assessment of penalties for any violations under all of the federal environmental statutes that EPA administers, and supersedes any inconsistent provisions in media-specific penalty or enforcement policies and EPA's 1986 Environmental Auditing Policy Statement.

(2) To the extent that existing EPA enforcement policies are not inconsistent, they will continue to apply in conjunction with this policy. However, a regulated entity that has received penalty mitigation for satisfying specific conditions under this policy may not receive additional penalty mitigation for satisfying the same or similar conditions under other policies for the same violation(s), nor will this policy apply to violations which have received penalty mitigation under other policies.

(3) This policy sets forth factors for consideration that will guide the Agency in the exercise of its prosecutorial discretion. It states the Agency's views as to the proper allocation of its enforcement resources. The policy is not final agency action, and is intended as guidance. It does not create any rights, duties, obligations, or defenses, implied or otherwise, in any third parties.

(4) This policy should be used whenever applicable in settlement negotiations for both administrative and civil judicial enforcement actions. It is not intended for use in pleading, at hearing or at trial. The policy may be applied at EPA's discretion to the settlement of administrative and judicial enforcement actions instituted prior to, but not yet resolved, as of the effective date of this policy.

H. Public Accountability

(1) Within 3 years of the effective date of this policy, EPA will complete a study of the effectiveness of the policy in encouraging:

(a) changes in compliance behavior within the regulated community, including improved compliance rates;

(b) prompt disclosure and correction of violations, including timely and accurate compliance with reporting requirements;

(c) corporate compliance programs that are successful in preventing violations, improving environmental performance, and promoting public disclosure;

(d) consistency among state programs that provide incentives for voluntary compliance.

EPA will make the study available to the public.

(2) EPA will make publicly available the terms and conditions of any compliance agreement reached under this policy, including the nature of the violation, the remedy, and the schedule for returning to compliance.

I. Effective Date

This policy is effective January 22, 1996.

Dated: December 18, 1995.

Steven A. Herman,

Assistant Administrator for Enforcement and Compliance Assurance.

[FR Doc. 95-31146 Filed 12-21-95; 8:45 am]

NOTICES

ENVIRONMENTAL PROTECTION AGENCY

[FRL-5976-6]

EPA Position Statement on Environmental Management Systems and ISO 14001 and a Request for Comments on the Nature of the Data To Be Collected From Environmental Management System/ISO 14001 Pilots

Thursday, March 12, 1998

*12094 AGENCY: Environmental Protection Agency.

ACTION: Position statement; request for comment on information gathering.

SUMMARY: This document communicates the EPA's position regarding Environmental Management Systems (EMSs), including those based on the International Organization for ***12095** Standardization (ISO) 14001 standard. This document also describes the evaluative stage EPA is entering concerning EMSs. Further, it solicits comments on proposed categories of information to be collected from a variety of sources that will provide data for a public policy evaluation of EMSs.

FOR FURTHER INFORMATION CONTACT:

Office of Reinvention — EMS, Environmental Protection Agency, 401 M St., SW, mail code 1803, Washington, D.C. 20460, Telephone: (202) 260-4261. E-mail: reinvention@epamail.epa.gov.

SUPPLEMENTARY INFORMATION:

I. Background

A diverse group of organizations, associations, private corporations and governments has been developing and implementing various EMS frameworks for the past thirty years. For example, the Chemical Manufacturers Association created its own framework called Responsible Care. In addition, the French, Irish, Dutch, and Spanish governments developed their own voluntary EMS standards.

The possibility that these diverse EMS frameworks could result in barriers to international trade led to a heightened interest in formulating an international voluntary standard for EMSs. To that end, the International Organization for Standardization (ISO), consisting of representatives from industry, government, non-governmental organizations (NGOs), and other entities, finalized the ISO 14001 EMS standard in September 1996. The intent of this standard is to produce a single framework for EMSs, which can accommodate varied applications all over the world. ISO 14001 is unique among the ISO 14000 standards because it can be objectively audited against for internal evaluation purposes or for purposes of self-declaration or third-party certification of the system.

EPA participation in the development of voluntary standards, including the ISO 14000 series of standards, is consistent with the goals reflected in section 12(d) of the National Technology Transfer and Advancement Act of 1995 (NTTAA) (Pub. L. No. 104-113, s. 12(d), 15 U.S.C. 272 note). The NTTAA requires federal agencies to use voluntary consensus standards in certain activities as a means of carrying out policy objectives or other activities determined by the agencies, unless the use of these standards would be inconsistent with applicable law or otherwise impractical. In addition, agencies must participate in the development of voluntary standards when such participation is in the public interest and is compatible with an agency's mission, authority, priority, and budget resources. Agency participation in the development of EMS voluntary standards does not necessarily connote EPA's agreement with, or endorsement of, such voluntary standards.

On December 16, 1997, EPA Deputy Administrator Fred Hansen asked EPA's newly chartered Office of Reinvention "to take lead responsibility for policy coordination of all EMS pilots, programs, and communications." (Full text of memo available at www.epa.gov/reinvent.) This notice initiates the Office of Reinvention's effort to ensure public input in that endeavor.

II. Statement

Implementation of an EMS has the potential to improve an organization's environmental performance and compliance with regulatory requirements. EPA supports and will help promote the development and use of EMSs, including those based on the ISO 14001 standard, that help an organization achieve its environmental obligations and broader environmental performance goals. In doing so, EPA will work closely with all key stakeholders, especially our partners in the States.

EPA encourages the use of EMSs that focus on improved environmental performance and compliance as well as source reduction (pollution prevention) and system performance. EPA supports efforts to develop quality data on the performance of any EMS to determine the extent to which the system can help bring about improvements in these areas. EPA also encourages organizations that develop EMSs to do so through an open and inclusive process with relevant stakeholders, and to maintain accountability for the performance outcomes of their EMSs through measurable objectives and targets. EPA encourages organizations to make information on the actual performance of their environmental management systems available to the public and governmental agencies. In addition, through initiatives such as Project XL and the Environmental Leadership Program, EPA is encouraging the testing of EMSs to achieve superior environmental performance. At this time, EPA is not basing any regulatory incentives solely on the use of EMSs, or certification to ISO 14001.

The Commission for Environmental Cooperation (CEC) Council issued on June 12, 1997, a resolution (#97-05) signed by EPA Deputy Administrator Fred Hansen on behalf of the United States concerning "future cooperation regarding environmental management systems and compliance." The CEC Council was formed pursuant to the North American Agreement on Environmental Cooperation, an environmental side agreement to the North American Free Trade Agreement, and is comprised of the environmental ministers for Canada, Mexico and the United States. The declarative and directive paragraphs of the Council's resolution #97-05 read as follows:

The Council * * * Declares That:

Governments must retain the primary role in establishing environmental standards and verifying and enforcing compliance with laws and regulations. Strong and effective governmental programs to enforce environmental laws and regulations are essential to ensure the protection of public health and the environment. Voluntary compliance programs and initiatives developed by governments can supplement strong and effective enforcement of environmental laws and regulations, can encourage mutual trust between regulated entities and government, and can facilitate the achievement of common environmental protection goals; Private voluntary efforts, such as adoption of Environmental Management Systems (EMSs) such as those based on the International Organization on Standardization's Specification Standard 14001 (ISO 14001), may also foster improved environmental compliance and sound environmental management and performance. ISO 14001 is not, however, a performance standard. Adoption of an EMS pursuant to ISO 14001 does not constitute or guarantee compliance with legal requirements and will not in any way prevent the governments from taking enforcement actions where appropriate;

HEREBY DIRECTS:

The Working Group to explore (1) the relationship between the ISO 14000 series and other voluntary EMSs to government programs to enforce, verify and promote compliance with environmental laws and regulations, and (2) opportunities to exchange information and develop cooperative positions regarding the role and effect of EMSs on compliance and other environmental performance. The Working Group shall, no later than the 1998 Council Session, report its results to the Council and provide recommendations for future cooperative action in this area. The review and recommendations shall recognize and respect each Party's domestic requirements and sovereignty.

III. Evaluative Phase

EPA is working in partnership with a number of states to explore the utility of EMSs, especially those based substantially on ISO 14001, in public policy innovation. The goal of this partnership is to gather credible and compatible information of known quality adequate to address key public policy issues. The primary mechanism *12096 to generate this information will be pilot projects. Valid, compatible data from other sources will also be used whenever possible. To make efficient use of resources, and to ensure more robust research, EPA and states will work together on the creation of a common data base. The data base will be open and usable, while recognizing the need to insure the appropriate level of confidentiality for participants.

A group of federal and state officials involved in EMS pilot projects have been working together to set up a common national database of information gathered through the pilot projects. As part of that process, EPA and states are developing a series of data protocols which provide instructions and survey instruments to guide the actual collection of data for the data base. That document will be available at http://www.epa.gov/reinvent.

This document will serve to solicit comments on the categories of information to be collected. From the following general categories of information (and possibly others), EPA and participating states will develop the above mentioned protocols.

The following categories are designed to provide a general idea as to the types of information that EPA believes should be collected to evaluate the effectiveness of EMSs from the perspective of regulators. EPA further believes that collection of data in all categories will allow the fullest understanding and evaluation of the benefits of an EMS. The data categories which appear in this document were, to the extent possible, developed around the kinds of data we believe will or could be generated by an ISO 14001 EMS.

1. Environmental Performance

The impact a facility has on the environment is of paramount importance to regulators' assessment of EMSs. Thus, it is critical to measure any change in a facility's environmental performance that might be attributable to implementation of an EMs. Information would be collected as to the types, amounts, and properties of pollutants that are released to air, surface water, groundwater, or the land. Information on these pollutants would need to be normalized to a facility's production levels. Information relating to recycling, reuse, and energy requirements could also be included. This inquiry could include both regulated and non-regulated pollutants.

2. Compliance

Implementation of an EMS has the potential to improve an organization's environmental compliance with regulatory requirements. The goal of collecting compliance information is to be able to measure the relationship between an EMs and compliance with local, state and federal environmental regulations. The types of data to be collected would include: information on whether the facility has a recent history of regulatory violations; the number, and seriousness of the violations; how quickly violations were discovered and corrected; and measurements of any changes in regulatory compliance status.

3. Pollution Prevention

Pollution prevention is a significant goal for both federal and state regulators. Therefore, better understanding the relationship between an organization's overall performance and the role of pollution prevention in the organization's EMs is important to regulators. In the federal context, pollution prevention is defined as "* * * any practice which — (1) reduces the amount of any hazardous substance, pollutant, or contaminant entering any waste stream, or otherwise released into the environment (including fugitive emissions) prior to recycling, treatment, or disposal; and (ii) reduces the hazards to public health and the environment associated with the release of such substances, pollutants, or contaminants." [FN1] This definition will likely serve as a basis for helping an organization identify measures that it might have taken towards pollution prevention. Data collected would include a description of the type of pollution prevention and source reduction techniques used, including good operating practices, inventory control, spill and leak prevention, raw material modification/substitution, process modification, and product reformulation or redesign.

FN1 Pollution Prevention Act of 1990 Section 6603, 42 U.S.C. 13102 (1990).

4. Environmental Conditions

In order to understand the impact of an EMs on the environment, it is necessary to know something about the status of the ambient environment surrounding the facility prior to implementation of an EMS. An analysis of this nature will not only help regulators evaluate EMs, it should also help facility mangers prioritize their environmental aspects and shape the policies and objectives of their EMSs. Environmental conditions data will assist all parties in determining the sustainability of certain human activities from an environmental, economic and social perspective. It is difficult, of course, to collect accurate and comparable information about environmental conditions. The time and expense needed for a facility to collect and report such data could be prohibitive. Also, the selection of an appropriate geographic focus — local, regional, or global — will be challenging. One way to minimize this burden would be to utilize available governmental or other surveys (e.g., the 1990 U.S. Census, hydrogeologic reports). Nevertheless, to the degree that these obstacles can be overcome, the analysis conducted by federal and state regulators will benefit.

5. Costs/Benefits to Impelementing Facilities

There has been much speculation and assertion about the relative costs and benefits associated with the implementation of an EMS. Data collected in this category should help provide answers to questions concerning possible net financial benefits that might accompany improved compliance and increased environmental performance, or that might result from being able to achieve compliance in less costly ways. The data may also shed light on the costs associated with higher levels of environmental performance. It is important to recognize some of the limitations inherent in traditional approaches to cost/benefit analysis. To address these limitations, organizations could be encouraged to identify intangible costs and benefits associated with the implementation of an EMS, even if they are difficult to quantify. Also, a list of usually "hidden" costs and benefits could be used to help organizations identify and understand costs and benefits that are traditionally overlooked.

6. Stakeholder Participation and Confidence

Community participation has become an increasingly important component of federal and state efforts to increase environmental performance and protect human health. Both federal and state regulators are interested in understanding the involvement of local communities and other stakeholders in the EMS process. Data could be collected to assess the amount and degree of stakeholder participation in both the development and implementation of an organization's EMS, or the effect that such participation has on the public credibility of the facility's EMS implementation.

More information concerning the pilot projects as well as other federal, state and international initiatives relating to *12097 EMSs and ISO 14000 can be found in the ISO 14000 Resource Directory (copies can be obtained through EPA's Pollution Prevention Information Clearinghouse at 202-260-1023, e-mail: ppic @epamail.epa.gov).

Dated: March 6, 1998.

Fred Hansen,

Deputy Administrator.

[FR Doc. 98-6389 Filed 3-11-98; 8:45 am]

ISO 14000 by Jack Kanholm

ISO 14001 ENVIRONMENTAL SYSTEM MANUAL AND PROCEDURES

Book and computer software with quality manual, procedures and forms - $ 290.

This computer software is a unique resource for documenting an ISO 14001 environmental system. It offers:

- An environmental management system that satisfies certification requirements and is sensitive to regulatory and legal issues.
- Fully developed two-level documentation, including the environmental manual, procedures and forms.
- Computer templates for procedures and forms (in Microsoft Word or WordPerfect).

It is compatible with Jack Kanholm's ISO 9000 system.

ISO 14001 REQUIREMENTS

61 Requirements Checklist and Compliance Guide

138 Pages
Hardcover Book - $ 49.

ISO 14001 IN OUR COMPANY

Self-Study Course for Personnel

32-Page Booklet, Test and Certificate - $ 9.

This book identifies 61 distinct, auditable requirements in ISO 14001. Each requirement is systematically explained with regard to interpretation, procedures, records, evidence of conformance and relevant auditing practices. In essence, the book reinterprets the standards into a list of 61 specific actions that need to be taken to achieve conformance, and explains how to implement them in the organization. A truly unique reference.

This is a general orientation course for ISO 14001.The workbook is intended for distribution to all personnel for self-study or group training. The course explains what the ISO 14000 standards are, how the environmental management system works, and how everyone should prepare themselves and their work areas for the certification audit. The course includes a short test and a certificate of completion, to satisfy the requirement for training records.

ISO 14000 and the Law   S. Wayne Rosenbaum

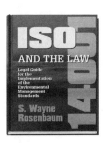

ISO 14001 AND THE LAW

Legal Guide for the Implementation of the Environmental Management Standards

168 Pages, Hardcover, $ 59.

In this book, Mr. Rosenbaum systematically identifies the legal issues and pitfalls associated with implementing ISO 14001, and offers practical tips and strategies to mitigate these legal risks. In plain language the book explains how the law and ISO 14001 interact, and how this may result in changing an organization's legal exposure. There is also a discussion of legal aspects for registrars and auditors. The book is intended for corporate managers and implementation teams, and for auditors, registrars, regulators and environmental attorneys.

More info on the internet at www.AQAco.com

ISO 13485 & EN 46000
by Lynette Howard and Jack Kanholm

ISO 13485 (EN 46000) QUALITY SYSTEM MANUAL AND 36 PROCEDURES

Book and computer software with quality manual, procedures and forms - $ 390.

ISO 13485 (EN 46000) REQUIREMENTS

99 Requirements Checklist and Compliance Guide

170 Pages
Hardcover Book - $ 59.

ISO 13485 (EN 46000) IN OUR COMPANY

Self-Study Course for Personnel

32-Page Booklet, Test and Certificate - $ 9.

QUALITY SYSTEM FOR THE MEDICAL DEVICE INDUSTRY

The three publications in this series provide: ready-made template documentation with the quality manual and operational procedures, explanation of all ISO 13485 and EN 46000 requirements, and a general orientation course for personnel. All three publications are based on Jack Kanholm's ISO 9000 series (refer to the preceding page annotating the ISO 9000 publications).

Ms. Howard contributed her unique knowledge of both the U.S. and European regulatory requirements and certification systems.

QS-9000 by Jack Kanholm

QS-9000 QUALITY SYSTEM MANUAL AND 40 PROCEDURES

Book and computer software with quality manual, procedures and forms - $ 390.

QS-9000 REQUIREMENTS

107 Requirements Checklist and Compliance Guide

177 Pages
Hardcover Book - $ 59.

QS-9000 IN OUR COMPANY

Self-Study Course for Personnel

32-Page Booklet, Test and Certificate - $ 9.

QUALITY SYSTEM FOR THE AUTOMOTIVE INDUSTRY

The three publications in this series provide: ready-made template documentation with the quality manual and operational procedures, explanation of all QS-9000 requirements, and a QS-9000 general orientation course for personnel. All three publications are based on Jack Kanholm's ISO 9000 series (refer to the preceding page annotating the ISO 9000 publications).

Since 1995 thousands of companies have used these materials to successfully achieve QS-9000 certification.

More info on the internet at www.AQAco.com

O R D E R   F O R M

Qty	Title	Prc	Dsc	Total	Qty	Title	Prc	Dsc	Total
	ISO 9000					**ISO 14000**			
	ISO 9000 Requirements	$ 49.	%			ISO 14001 Requirements	$ 49.	%	
	ISO 9000 Quality System	$ 69.	%			ISO 14001 And The Law	$ 59.	%	
	ISO 9000 In Our Company	$ 9.	%			ISO 14001 In Our Company	$ 9.	%	
	ISO 9000 Template Manual and Procedures Software	$ 290.	%			ISO 14001 Template Manual and Procedures Software	$ 290.	%	
	QS-9000					**ISO 13485 (EN 46000)**			
	QS-9000 Requirements	$ 59.	%			ISO 13485 Requirements	$ 59.	%	
	QS-9000 In Our Company	$ 9.	%			ISO 13485 In Our Company	$ 9.	%	
	QS-9000 Template Manual and Procedures Software	$ 390.	%			ISO 13485 Template Manual and Procedures Software	$ 390.	%	

Sales tax of 7.75% (CA only) and shipping cost (see chart below) will be added to invoice

Quantity Discounts (copies per title)

5 to 9:	10%	20 to 39: 30%	Over 100: 50%
10 to 19:	20%	40 to 99: 40%	

Shipping (by UPS)

❏ Ground $ 6.   ❏ 2nd Day $ 13.
❏ 3rd Day $ 9.   ❏ Next Day $ 25.

Shipping Address (No PO Boxes)

Mr. ❏   Ms. ❏ _____

Title: _____

Company: _____

Street: _____

City: _____ State: _____ Zip: _____

Phone & Fax: _____

Billing Address

Company: _____

Street: _____

City: _____ State: _____ Zip: _____

Attention: _____

Method of Payment

Card No.: |_|_|_|_|_|_|_|_|_|_|_|_|_|_|_|_|

❏ Check ❏ Visa ❏ MC ❏ AmEx   Exp.: _____

❏ Bill Company Purchase Order No.: _____

Signature & Date: _____

30 Day Preview

❏ Yes, I want to preview the publications and reserve the right to return them for a refund (excluding shipping cost), if not satisfied.
I understand that to receive a refund, I must return the publications within 30 days.

To order, fax this form to (626) 796 9070 or call (800) 600 3601

ISO 14001 AND THE LAW